To George Shaw
with thanks for
your help in making
the publication of this
book possible
from Ron Kerridge.

# A HISTORY OF LANCING

# A
# history of
# LANCING

## R. G. P. KERRIDGE

PHILLIMORE

1979

Published by
PHILLIMORE & CO., LTD.
London and Chichester
*Head Office*: Shopwyke Hall,
Chichester, Sussex, England

ISBN 0 85033 338 5

Printed in England by
COASBYPRINT LIMITED
Portsmouth, Hampshire

and bound by
THE NEWDIGATE PRESS LTD.
at Book House, Dorking, Surrey

# CONTENTS

## LIST OF PLATES
*(between pages 80 and 81)*

# LIST OF FIGURES

## LIST OF MAPS

## DIAGRAMS

# ACKNOWLEDGEMENTS

Acknowledgements are made in particular to the following:

The County Archivist, Mrs. P. Gill, at the West Sussex Record Office, Chichester, for her kind permission to use extracts and notes from the Enclosure and Tithe Maps and Awards of Lancing and the Overseer's Records for the parish. Several references are made throughout the book. Also I am indebted for the valuable advice and assistance given to me by Mrs. Gill and her staff throughout my researches.

Mr. B. W. T. Handford for his kind permission for the use of extracts from his articles in the College magazines of the 1950s and for the use of the address given to the Friends of the Chapel in 1970. Also for his valuable knowledge and assistance given to me over the years.

The British Library for kind permission to use a copy of a drawing of Lancing Manor in 1789 by Grimm, from the Burrell collection.

Lady Egremont, on behalf of her son, for permission to use the information from a map of the salt marshes in Lancing (Petworth House Archives, 3263).

I am also indebted to the following who have assisted me in many ways during my research:
Mr. K. W. Dickins, ex curator of Deeds, Sussex Archaeological Society, Barbican House, Lewes; Dr. G. W. Shaw of Lancing College; the late Mr. T. Walton; Mr. M. Norman, curator of the Marlipins Museum, Shoreham; Mr. S. Easter; Mr. R. Elleray; Dr. Hudson, at present (1978) working on the *V.C.H.*

Also to all those people, too numerous to mention individually, who have helped in providing photographic and other relevant material.

# PREFACE

At the present time, Lancing, together with a very few other local coastal parishes, shares the distinction of having no published history, even though it is now a popular seaside resort during the summer. One of the reasons for the apparent lack of interest in the parish may be the fact that information has to be painstakingly searched for and extracted from many scattered sources throughout the county and even from several sources outside it. Although no major events have taken place in Lancing to make it famous, it nevertheless has an interesting history.

During the past seven years that I have been carrying out research, an increasing interest has been shown in the history of the locality.

I have now been urged by many people to publish my findings, and therefore this book is dedicated to those people, who, like myself, find Lancing and its district an interesting place. I do not propose to exclude, however, those people who are new to Lancing, those merely curious about its history, or indeed the children of today who may wish to know more about the parish.

I do not pretend that this book is by any means a complete history of the parish, but more of a contribution towards it. I have not tried to deal specifically with how the events of history affected the way of life of the people of Lancing, but have attempted to weld together the information which I have gathered, collated and analysed over the years.

Worthing, 1978                                          R. G. P. KERRIDGE

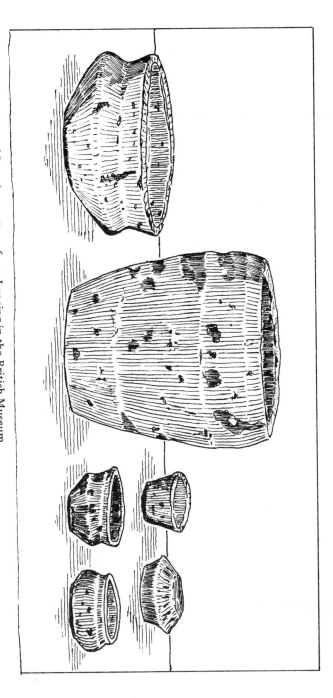

Fig. 1. Bronze Age and Iron Age pottery from Lancing in the British Museum.

Fig. 2. The Roman Temple site at Lancing, 1828. (Based on a drawing from *Collectanea Antiqua*, Vol. 1, 1843.)

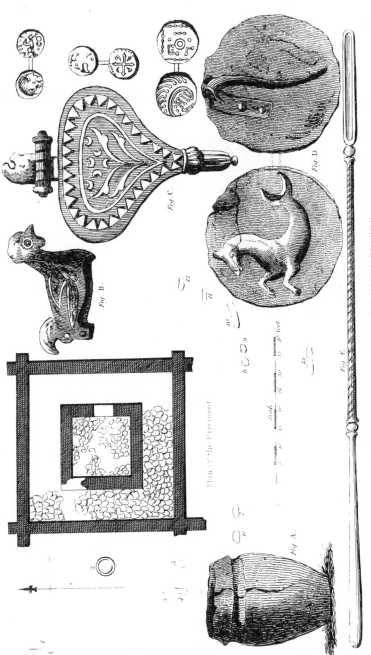

Fig. 3. Roman remains on Lancing Down, Sussex.

Fig. 4. Lancing Manor House as it was in 1789 (based on a drawing by Grimm— by kind permission of the British Library Board).

*Chapter One*

## LANCING, ANCIENT AND MODERN

THE MODERN parish of Lancing in the county of Sussex is situated on the coastal plain between Sompting and Shoreham, and is bordered on the north by the parish of Coombes and on the south by the English Channel. It is a popular seaside resort in the summer, and is in direct communication by road and rail with Worthing, three miles to the west, and Brighton, eight miles to the east. The area of the parish is 2,236 acres. The village of Lancing is without doubt of Saxon origin, but the surrounding area has provided evidence of life from much earlier times.

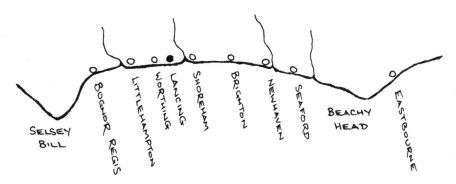

Fig. 5. The position of Lancing

The ancient track, which passes Lancing Ring (locally known as Lancing Clump) and then down past Hoe Court cottages via

1

the north side of the chalk-pit and on to the *Sussex Pad* inn, is considered to be of Neolithic origin. The track, which approaches Lancing Ring from the side of Steepdown on the north is, in fact, a branch of the ridgeway which runs from Beachy Head to Hampshire and Salisbury Plain. North of Lancing Ring the track passes over the site of a small Romano-Celtic temple and then on to Steepdown. One part of the track branches off to Cissbury, while the other proceeds to Chanctonbury and on to the west.

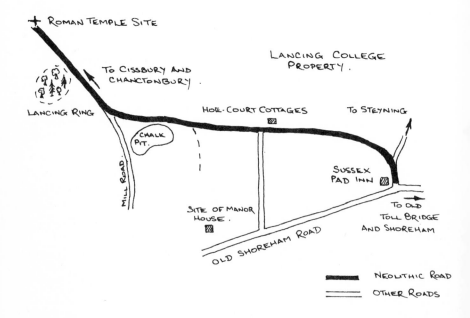

Fig. 6. Showing course of Neolithic road

In the vicinity of Lancing Hill, west of the College, dumps of 'pot-boilers' have been found and this hill is locally known as Boiler Hill.

In 1929 an Acheulian hand-axe made of flint was found in a deposit of clay on the surface of a ploughed field about a hundred yards east of Lancing College chapel, by a Mr. H. R. Hickman. In 1931 Dr. Eliot Curwen, F.S.A., examined the specimen and described it as 'A blunt pointed ovate hand-axe of the St. Acheul section of the Lower (or Drift) division of the Palaeolithic period . . .'.[1]

 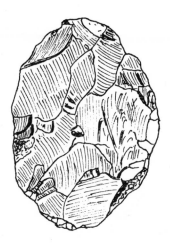

Fig. 7. Acheulian hand-axe from Lancing College. (Approx. half full size). (Based on a drawing in S.A.C., Vol. 81, p. 143)

There are five flint scrapers classed as Neolithic in the Museum of Archaeology and Ethnology, Cambridge, of which three came from Lancing Ring and two from 'near Lancing Station', and in Worthing Museum is a flint sickle blade which was found in the brick-earth at Lancing, south of the railway.

Lack of adequate records makes it difficult to place the exact location of Bronze Age finds. However, the British Museum possesses an incense cup, two bowls and a biconical urn 'from Lancing', classed as Middle Bronze Age. The Pitt-Rivers Museum in Oxford contains a small urn and bowl 'from Lancing', described as Late Bronze Age, whilst the Ashmolean Museum, Oxford, holds a small vessel of overhanging rim-type from the Middle Bronze Age. (These Bronze Age vessels are all illustrated in *S.A.C.,* Vol. 81, pp. 147–8).

The site of the Romano-Celtic temple lies across the Neolithic track to the north of Lancing Ring. The ruins were discovered on Good Friday 1828 by J. Medhurst, who had been carrying out researches on the South Downs for the

Fig. 8. Middle Bronze Age urn in the Ashmolean Museum, Oxford. (Based
on a photograph in *S.A.C.*, Vol. 81, page 148.)

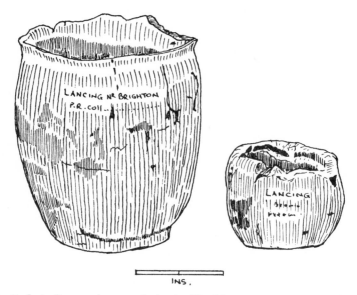

Fig. 9. Late Bronze Age vessels in the Pitt-River Museum, Oxford. (Based
on a photograph in *S.A.C.*, Vol. 81, page 148.)

previous nine years. The whole of the site was covered by a four foot high mound which gave the appearance of an ancient barrow of considerable size. When the centre of the mound was penetrated to a depth of about four feet, Medhurst came to a pavement 40 feet square with a room 16 feet square in the centre. The walls of the building were of flint and about two feet thick; the remains of the walls were level with the ground except in a few places where they rose to a height of about two feet, and the sides were plastered and coloured red. The floors were of coarse tesserae, undecorated and laid in mortar on a bed of flints. Upon the floors were ashes and rubbish suggesting that the building was destroyed by fire. Around the site were several graves from which were obtained ashes, rudely carved combs, fibulae and some pottery.

Mr. Medhurst, who was formerly a turner in Brighton, laid open the site and cordoned it off. He erected a hut on the site in which he exhibited the items recovered from the area, and a small water-colour of this hut is shown in Worthing Museum. A notice was posted at the site offering Mr. Medhurst's thanks to the visitors, informing them of the admission charge (adults one shilling, and children sixpence), and of the fact that he would be in attendance from 8 a.m. till seven in the evening!

Several coins were found on the site which date the temple from the 1st to the 3rd century. In *The Archaeology of Sussex*, E. Cecil Curwen states that votive offerings to the local deity were usually to be found within these temple sites, mainly in the form of coins, although on the Continent they often took the form of Neolithic flint axes or sea urchin fossils. Apparently these temples were peculiar to southern Britain and Gaul and were situated on hilltops. They were dedicated to local deities who were sometimes identified with the classical Mercury, Apollo and Mars. However, in 1833, Medhurst, for no apparent reason, grubbed up every possible piece of the building from the site and removed it to his house in North Lancing, to exhibit.[2] The location of this house is as yet unknown. Figure 3, taken from the *Gentleman's Magazine*, July 1830, shows some of the objects found on the site of the temple.

Although the Ordnance Survey maps later recognised the site, it was originally marked incorrectly, as suspected by Professor Haverfield, a classics master at Lancing College. In 1929 L. A. Biddle and B. W. T. Handford from the College re-discovered the correct site and, not knowing at that time that the site had been plundered 100 years earlier, had to be content with collecting all the broken pottery they could find before abandoning the site. The modern Ordnance Survey maps show the correct position of the site.[3]

Other finds of broken glass and small objects of Roman date were made in the garden of 'Shadwells', which was at the eastern end of The Street in North Lancing. The name of the 'Street' commemorates the suspected Roman road from Chichester across the coastal plain through Sompting and Lancing to the ford at the River Adur where the modern *Sussex Pad* inn stands.

As previously mentioned, the settlement of Lancing is of Saxon origin. One person possibly associated with its beginnings is Wlencing, the son of Aelle, the Saxon chieftain. It is recorded in the *Anglo-Saxon Chronicle* that Aelle landed in 'Brytenland' in A.D. 477, together with his three sons, Cymen, Wlencing, and Cissa. After slaying many Britons, it is suggested that Wlencing established himself at a site known later as Lancing, i.e., North Lancing. Another group settled further to the east to form the Manor of How (pronounced 'Hoe'), now Hoe Court. By the time the boundaries of the manors were settled, probably by the end of the 7th century A.D., there were two principal settlements in the area, Lancing and How, both of which now form the modern parish of Lancing.

In 1928 a Saxon cemetery of the 6th century was unearthed at Hoe Court House. Six burial sites were examined, three of which produced iron weapons in the form of spearheads and knives. Later, in 1936, further examinations were made which resulted in the discovery of a seventh burial, believed to be of a slightly later date than the former six.[4]

In November 1971 an archaeological dig was carried out in part of the old marshlands, now part of New Monks Farm. While ploughing this land the owner of the farm noticed a number of oyster shells accompanied by several mounds dotted about the area. The dig confirmed that they were sites of Saxon salt pans of about the 10th century, and the presence of some fragments of pottery known as Porchester Ware enabled the excavators to fix a fairly accurate date. The manufacture of salt was a regular practice of the Saxons all along the coastal plain, and it continued for several hundred years after them. The salt pans were no doubt some of those mentioned in the Domesday Book for Lancing and How.

Fig. 10. Saxon inhumation, Hoe Court House, North Lancing

From research carried out over the years and information contained in early records and later in maps of the 17th and 18th centuries, it is possible to put together a picture of early Lancing.

Lancing was bordered on the west by the great expanse of water which flowed up to Sompting and Broadwater from the sea; this water was known as the Broad Water, from which the village of the same name originated. It has been suggested that boats sailed up to Sompting and anchored there. The remains of the Broad Water can at present be seen as the low-lying land to the south of Sompting and at Decoy Farm, which in 1978 was being used as a refuse tip. The Teville stream running through the area is all that remains of the original great expanse of water.

To the south of Lancing is the English Channel, while on the east is the River Adur, known then as the Bramber Water or Aqua de Brembre. The area of marshland in Lancing repre-- sented by the modern airport, Old and New Salts Farms, and New Monks Farm, was then the large estuary of the River Adur. Indeed, silt and other deposits found during the archaeological dig in 1971 indicate that the water flowed in a south-westerly direction from the *Sussex Pad* and emerged into the open sea in the vicinity of the modern Shopsdam Road area.

The old road to Steyning from the *Sussex Pad* via Coombes was once an early west river bank, while the old Shoreham Road from the Manor was the north bank. Fingers of water from this estuary reached along the side of the road to opposite Lancing Manor and many years later the Fresh brook reached out to Grinstead Lane. Thus it can be seen that Lancing was represented as a narrow peninsular. The way in which Lancing developed, the various field names and other later records which are dealt with in later chapters certainly give weight to this theory.

The study of place-names is a fascinating subject full of pitfalls and the exact origin of Lancing is as difficult as any to pinpoint.

There is no doubt that places ending in 'ing' mean 'the people of' and hence Professor Ekwall says that Wlencingas is undoubtedly a derivative of the personal name Wlencing and Roberts agrees with this,[5] while Mawer and Stenton[6] suggest that it may have been derived from other name stems such as Wlanc, meaning 'proud' or 'imperious', of Hlanc, 'lank' or 'lean', and that the history of the word may have been affected by the common word 'lance', in use well before 1290.

The spelling of the word Lancing from the time of Domesday shows nearly every conceivable way of conveying the place name. It is most likely that the variations are due only to errors in transcriptions and each writer's individual attempt to reproduce his version of the pronunciation of the word Lancing. The list which follows shows many of these variations of spellings taken from various sources.

It is interesting to note that one of the nearest spellings to that of the modern word occurs in the Domesday Book.

| Date | Spelling | Date | Spelling |
|------|----------|------|----------|
| 1086 | Lancinges[9] | 1361 | Lanceyng[5] |
| 1235 | (South) Launcynges[7] | 1377 | Launsynge[5] |
| 1242 | Lanzinges[6] | 1384 | Lanncynge[13] |
| 1262 | Launching[6] | 1385 | Lainsyngge[6] |
| 1263 | Launcynges[7] | 1395 | Launcyng[7] |
| 1271 | Launchynge[7] | 1404 | Lansynge[6] |
| 1274 | Launcyng[5] | 1413 | Lancinges[7] |
| 1278 | Launcinges[5] | 1497 | Launsyng[7] |
| 1296 | (North) Launcynges[6] | 1503 | Launsyng[5] |
| 1296 | Lancyng[10] | 1524 | Lawensyng[8] |
| 1316 | Launcing[5] | 1568 | Lawnsinge[14] |
| c. 1320 | Langinges[5] | 1595 | Lawnsinge[6] |
| 1320 | Lazinges[5] | | |
| 1327 | Launcyng[11] | 1627 | Launsinge[15] |
| 1332 | Launcyng[12] | 1641 | Launsing[16] |
| 1354 | Launcynge[7] | 1705 | Lanceing[17] |
| 1359 | Launcyng[7] | Present day | Lancing |

The boundaries of ancient Lancing were very similar to those of the modern parish which is bordered on the north by Coombes, on the west by Sompting, on the south by the English Channel, and on the east by the River Adur. The two settlements of Lancinges and How mentioned in the Domesday Book comprise the parish of Lancing and total approximately 18 hides. Allowing 120 acres per hide, which is the commonly acceptable approximation for this area, we find that the parish was originally about 2,160 acres in extent. This figure is not much different from that of the present acreage of 2,236.

During the 17th, 18th and 19th centuries the course of the River Adur gradually moved eastwards. The river was continually creating successive new outlets into the sea by shingle banks which were forced into the river estuary from the west, due to the littoral drift of beach material. This eventually caused a right-angled bend eastwards in the river south of Shoreham, and for many years the river thus ran parallel to the sea before actually emptying into the sea at Portslade. The land to the south of this piece of the river was part of the parish of

Lancing. Even when a new artificial cut was made into the sea opposite Kingston in 1760 this land was still part of Lancing, although ownership was hotly disputed by the lord of the manor of Shoreham.

In 1838 the Tithe Award for Lancing shows the total acreage of the parish as 2,524, an increase of nearly three hundred acres on the present figure. However, most of this is accounted for by land south of the river at Shoreham and in 1910 a Local Government Board Order changed the eastern boundary of Lancing, placing this piece of land outside the parish of Lancing. The boundary thus ran down the low water mark of the River Adur from north to south and continued south-wards to the sea instead of following the river eastwards. This would put the boundary in a similar position to that of the ancient one, when the River Adur formerly flowed due south and emptied directly into the sea.

It is interesting to note that in 1868 there was a court case regarding this land south of the river, between the lords of the manors of Lancing and Shoreham (Carr-Lloyd *v.* Ingram). In his *History of Sussex* M. A. Lower has a footnote to the effect that the case was decided against the Lord of Lancing. However this would seem to be in error, or there may have been some other, later, transaction, for in 1889 land at Port-slade was sold to the Brighton and Hove Gas Co. by Lady Lloyd of Lancing. In 1907 the Shoreham and Lancing Land Co. purchased land from the Lloyd family estate, comprising Old and New Salts Farms with the foreshore from Semells Bridge (western boundary) to the harbour entrance, and from the harbour entrance to the gas works at Portslade, together with all manorial rights except that to remove shingle from the beach.

Old court rolls (records of the manorial courts) usually give details of 'beating the bounds' of the manors. This was in the form of a description of the walk around the manor boun-dary and signed by the bailiff of the manor. Lancing is no exception. The court rolls for the 'Manor of North Lancing and Monks, South Lancing and Lyons' which commence in 1677, do, in fact, describe the beating of the bounds, but there is one setback, namely that the rolls have disappeared.[18]

However, the transcript of the previously mentioned court case contains some extracts from these rolls and one concerns the 'beating of the bounds' of the manor.

During the trial in 1868 a certain Samuel Hampton, an inhabitant of Lancing, aged 68, and a shoemaker by trade, was called as a witness. He was asked to confirm the following extract from the manor rolls, which he did:

> A perambulation of the bounds of the Manor of North Lancing and Monks, South Lancing and Lyons, in the county of Sussex, the property of John Biddulph esquire as trod and gone by us, whose names are hereunder written this 9th day of August 1815; in pursuance of public notice inserted in the Lewes Journal and posted on the church doors of the Parishes adjoining the said manor. First, we set out from low water mark at Shoreham Bridge and followed the same low water mark down the river in its present course nearly as far as Kingston, where we found that, in consequence of the new cut made out of the old channel of the river into the sea, where piers were erected about the year 1760, and soon after blown up, the ancient course of the river had been diverted; we trod along low water mark at the former ancient course, leaving the present channel considerably to the south and we continued the said ancient course of the said river south until we came to the place where the old Harbour mouth was, previous to the cut of the aforesaid channel about the year 1760, and did run out into the sea, which was at a place which brought the east end of Aldrington Church in a line south from Post-lain, or Portslade windmill; from thence in the same line down to low water mark at sea following low water mark at sea as far as Lancing shops, then turning northwards under the west side of the bank as far as the water course following the water course in a south westerly direction to the beach within 40 yards of low water mark at sea; from thence we made a turn; then turning westwards at low water mark as far as west Sea Mill Bank where the western most boundary of this manor stands. Then turning northward along the west where the old bank crosses the highway to the beach . . .

Unfortunately the extract ends here, as the court was not interested in the Western or northern parts of the manor. However, a map of Lancing dated 1770[19] shows that the boundary continued due north to West Semell's Gate across to East Semell's Gate and the northwards along the modern Western Road, Boundstone Lane, Upper Boundstone Lane, and on up to the Downs to where it meets the old track from the chalk-pit

at the northern end of No-man's Land. From this point the
boundary runs eastwards separating Coombes and Lancing
parishes, along the Ladywell stream (north of Lancing College)
to the old Steyning road (from the *Sussex Pad*). From here it
runs along the road eastward to the sluice and stream at Cuckoo
Corner and out to the River Adur, where it runs southward
at low water mark, thus returning to the start at Shoreham
toll bridge. The total distance around the boundary was just
over eighteen and a half miles. During this walk a turn was made
at Lancing shops on the beach to walk around a very small
manor, known about a hundred years earlier as Wood's Manor
(the map of 1770 shows it as Poole's Manor).

Before we leave the subject of the boundaries a few amusing
incidents during the 'beating of the bounds' are worthy of
mention. Again, reverting to the court case of 1868, we find
witnesses describing incidents which were presumably not
recorded in the manor rolls. On one occasion a young lad,
who was one of the party 'treading the bounds', was thrown
into a ditch at a certain point in order to make him remember
on future occasions that this was a landmark to note carefully.
On another occasion, at a point where a change of direction
was necessary, a large letter 'B', representing J. Biddulph,
lord of the manor, was marked in the sand with a stick, and a
young member of the party had his rear banged onto the 'B'
to impress upon him and others that this was definitely part
of the property of the lord of the manor. It was also noted
that the party met before and after their task at the *Sussex Pad*
inn, where they were paid. Apparently most of them spent
their money at the inn, drinking and enjoying themselves for
several hours.

Some members of the 1815 party were Samuel Hampton,
John Hampton (father of Samuel), Richard Hampton (brother
of Samuel), John Carver, John Sharp, and William Holmes.
Other recorded dates of beating the bounds are: 27 June 1711;
26 July 1738; 31 August 1749; 9 October 1769; 1 July 1789;
9 August 1815; ? 1823; 25 September 1868; 24 March 1896;
and ? 1906.

*Chapter Two*

## MANORS, FARMS AND OTHER ESTATES

*The Manors of North and South Lancing*

AFTER the conquest of England in 1066 William reorganised Sussex and its six *rapes,* which ran north to south, each with its own river, castle and forest. William redistributed the Sussex estates by entrusting the rapes to some of his loyal noblemen. The Rape of Bramber, in which Lancing lies, was given to William de Braose. In the 10th century the Saxons had divided the county into *hundreds,* or tythings, which meant that each of these divisions held a hundred sureties to keep the King's peace. The hundred was a unit for taxation purposes and administering law and order. Lancing was described as being in the Rape of Bramber and the Hundred of Brightford.

The earliest record in which Lancing is positively identified is the Domesday Book from which the following entry is taken.[1]

> Robert holds Lancinges of William. Lewin held it of King Edward. It then vouched for 16 hides and one rod; of these Robert himself has 12 hides and one rod and they have paid geld for 5 hides and one rod and a half. There is land for 5 ploughs. In demesne are 2 ploughs and a half and 13 villeins and 7 bordars with 2 ploughs. There is 1 mill of 8 shillings, and 7 salterns of 20 shillings and 3 pence.
>
> Of this land 2 knights hold 2 hides and a half, and half a rod, and have 2 ploughs there in demesne and 11 salterns of 12 shillings and 6 pence. The whole in the time of King Edward was worth £9 and afterwards £7. Now £14 and 10 shillings.
>
> In the same vill Ralph holds 3 rods and a half; and they are part of the 16 hides above mentioned, and have paid geld for one rod. There is one villein and 2 bordars. Worth 5 shillings.
>
> Of the same manor another Ralph holds 3 hides and one rod, and they are also part of the above 16 hides. This land of Ralphs has

13

paid geld for 3 rods and does so now. In demesne is one plough, and
2 villeins and 2 bordars with half a plough. There are 5 salterns of
12 shillings and 6 pence. It is, and was, worth 50 shillings.
    And again, Ralph holds one rod, which lay in Lancinges, and
gave geld. One villein holds and held it. It is, and was, worth 5
shillings.

The William mentioned in the extract was William de Braose
and the Robert was Robert le Sauvage, Lord of Broadwater.
    The manor was sub-let at some date because its next mention
is when a William of Lancing died seized of it some time before
1206.[2] The manor was divided between his two daughters,
Bertha, wife of Nigel de Brok, and Alice, whose husband was
surnamed Malamaynes.
    The Malamaynes portion (or moiety) of the manor descended
through Alice's son and heir, Nicholas Malmeyns,[3] and his
younger son, Maurice, before 1219. John de Braose, who died
in 1232, had previously granted the mesne service of the
Malameynes share of Lancing manor to the Lord of Broadwater.[4] The 'Testa de Nevil', a record of the 13th century,
mentions a John de Gatesden, who held two knights' fees in
Lazinges (Lancing) with the heir of Maurice Malemaynes.[5]
(John de Gatesden married Hawys, the daughter of Robert le
Sauvage, in 1247).[6] In the 'Hundred Rolls' for Sussex, c. 1274,
it is said that 'the tything of Lancing was accustomed to perform suit to the hundred of Bredford [Brightford]; but with
consent of William de Braose the said tything was divided into
two parts, one of which performed suit at the court of the
Lord of Broadwater, and the other the the hundred of Bretford,
to the annual loss to the said hundred of 5s.'[7]
    The 'Testa de Nevil' also shows that a Ranulphus (Randulph)
de Brock also held two knights' fees in Langing (Lancing),
Alburn and Bungton.[5] This Randulph was lord of the de Brok
share of the Lancing manor. A Randulph de Brok was previously
lord in 1222, possibly a son of Bertha and Nigel de Brok.[8]
It appears that the two parts of Lancing manor were reunited
by the de Broks, possibly by Randulph.[9] However, the two
halves remained as distinct lordships, one to the Lord of Broadwater and the other to the Hundred of Brightford.[10] A further
mention of someone with the surname of de Brok in connection

with Lancing appears in the Papal Registers for 1263, where there are dispensations granted to Engeraud de Brok, chaplain to the Bishop of Porto, to hold the rectories of Angemere (Angmering) and Lancinges in the diocese of Lincoln.[11]

Another Nigel de Brok was lord of the manor between 1265 and 1279.[12] He was dead, however, by 1290, when his widow Christiana held Lancing.[13] By 1296 Thurstan de Brok was lord, and in 1299 his son Nigel. In 1315 was a final concord between Nigel de Brok and Matilda his wife, plaintiffs, and Thomas Avenal, deforcient, by which it was agreed that the manor of Lancing (two-thirds of which were held by the said Thomas, and the other third by Aveline, who was the wife of Dunstan de Brok), should be settled on Nigel and Matilda and their heirs, and if Nigel should die without issue, then on Matilda, the sister of Nigel, and, on failure of her issue, then on the right heirs of Nigel.[14]

It appears that Nigel died without issue, for Michael de Poynings held the manor in 1250, when he died,[15] and his wife, formerly Matilda de Brok, was probably the sister of Nigel. As there were no children by this marriage the manor reverted to the right heirs of Nigel and in 1361-2 his namesake was again lord of the manor.[16] By 1387 there appears to be no further mention of the name de Brok in connection with Lancing, but it is interesting to note that the historian Cartwright mentions that the de Brok family were of ancient descent and that they owned large estates in Lancing, Albourne and Buncton, probably from the time of Domesday and possibly before that. It is quite possible that one of the Christian names mentioned in the Domesday extract may have belonged to a member of the de Brok family.

The next mention of the manor occurs in 1400 when Richard Radmyld died seized of Lancing,[17] and in 1411-12 a survey of Sussex manors shows that his brother and heir, Ralph Radmyld, held 'Launsyng Manor', valued at £13.[18] From 1426 Lancing descended with the Broadwater portion of the manor held by the Radmyld family, and after 1457 the whole manor.[19] The manor then descended through the Radmyld family until the death of William Radmyld in 1499, which brought the male line of the family to an end. The Radmyld's manors of

Beverington, Broadwater, Alborne and Lancing, were all in the hands of feoffees by a grant of William Radmyld in 1497.[20] The manor has to be traced through the two aunts of William, namely Margaret and Isabella (daughters of Ralph Radmyld). Isabella had married Nicholas Lewkenor and had a son, Edward, whilst Margaret had married John Goring and had a son, John. Thus the sons, Edward Lewkenor and John Goring, became joint owners of the manor of Lancing and the manors of Broadwater, Albourne, and Beverington. It appears that they shared out these manors, and Lancing went to John Goring. The Goring family had already had connections with Lancing before acquiring the manor, since in 1362 John de Goring was shown as 'of Launcing' and for the next two generations a John Goring still resided there.[21]

In 1503, however, Lancing, together with the other Radmyld manors, came into the possession of George Neville, Lord Bergavenny. From this time there begins a series of complicated transactions with Westminster Abbey, concerning the purchase, by the Abbey, of certain manors in Nottinghamshire and Lincolnshire from Lord Bergavenny. The evidence contained in the Patent Rolls and Westminster Abbey muniments[22] shows that the manor of Lancing was transferred to the Abbey to create collateral security so that the Abbey could gain possession of the Nottinghamshire and Lincolnshire manors. In 1504, when the transactions were complete, Lancing manor returned to Lord Bergavenny; later in 1513 a fine shows '. . . the manor of Launcyng and tenements in Launcyng quit-claimed to plaintiffs and heirs of John Goring by George Nevile of Bergavenny, knight and Margaret his wife'.[23] So once more the manor returned to the Goring family, a branch of the family situated at Burton Park. The manor descended through the Goring family from father to son for over two hundred years until the death of Sir William Goring in 1725, when it descended to his great-nephew, Richard Biddulph, who died without any children, and so it passed to his brother, Charles Biddulph.

From 1553 onwards, after the death of an earlier Sir William Goring, the manor was described as 'North Lancing and Monks, South Lancing', apparently two separate manors now combined.

There is a probability that Monks *alias* South Lancing had a connection with members of the Monk family of the Middle Ages, to which there were a number of references.[24] It is, however, also likely that this name does in some way commemorate the small piece of land originally granted to the Monastery of Mottenden in Kent in 1350. The name of Monks, South Lancing, does not appear until after the execution of Thomas Cromwell in

BIDDULPH FAMILY

ARMS:- VERT, AN EAGLE, DISPLAYED, AR.

Fig. 11.

in 1541, who had obtained the Mottenden 'estate' in 1538. By the latter half of the 17th century the manor of Monks had become Monks Farm.

In the 19th century the farm was also known as the Manor Farm and the farmhouse was used to hold the Manorial Courts in Lancing. The farmhouse still exists, and is known as 'Monks Farm Presbytery'. The outhouses which once surrounded the house were removed to make way for the police station and flats. Part of the farmland which was situated to the west of the house is now maintained by the parish council, and is known as Monks Farm recreation ground.

The following list contains the known owners and occupiers of Monks Farm.

| Date | Owner | Occupier/Renter |
|------|-------|-----------------|
| 1692 | Sir William Goring | William Chatham |
| 1749 | Charles Biddulph | Edward Sowton |
| 1780–95 | Charles Biddulph/John Biddulph | John Weller |
| 1796–97 | John Biddulph | John Weller and Sarah Carver |
| 1798–1811 | John Biddulph | S. Carver and Lee |
| 1812–22 | John Biddulph | John Carver |
| 1823–27 | John Biddulph | N. Grinstead |
| 1828–31 | James Martin Lloyd | John Smith |

*continued*

*continued —*

| Date | Owner | Occupier/Renter |
|------|-------|-----------------|
| 1838 | James Martin Lloyd | John Streeter |
| 1855–58 | Lady Elizabeth Lloyd | Edwin Lucas |
| 1866–73 | G. K. Carr-Lloyd | Charles Stone |
| 1874 | G. K. Carr-Lloyd | Edwin Pronger |
| 1875 | G. K. Carr-Lloyd | H. Fawcett |
| 1876–79 | G. K. Carr-Lloyd/J. M. Carr-Lloyd | Edwin Pronger |
| 1895 | J. M. Carr-Lloyd | Adam Henry, Farm Bailiff to John Harrison |
| 1899–1912 | J. M. Carr-Lloyd | William Phillips |

From about 1770, however, other small manors in and around Lancing had united with the main manor of Lancing, and the combined manor was then known as 'North Lancing and Monks, South Lancing and Lyons' (this title remained until its dispersal in the 20th century). On Charles Biddulph's death in 1784 the manor descended to his son John, who also resided at Burton Park.

During the early part of the 18th century the Rev. James Lloyd, rector of Clapham, and descended from the ancient family of Lloyd of Halghton, Flint, came to Lancing. He died in 1721 and was buried in North Lancing churchyard. His son, James Lloyd, acquired the lease of the manor of How Court (Farm) in 1736-7 and farmed it. It is probable that he or his father lived in a cottage on the site of Lancing Manor House (demolished in 1972), as his memos regarding agricultural work at How Court mention going to How Court,[25] signifying that he lived elsewhere. At some date, *c.*1730, one of the Lloyd family had Lancing Manor House built around the site of the old cottage.

In 1789 a view of the house drawn by Grimm,[26] describes it as 'Mr Lloyds Cottage' (Fig. 4). It was probably added to and modernised several times over the years to become the Lancing Manor House, as most people knew it before it was demolished; indeed, in 1805 it was described as the 'mansion-house of Mr Lloyd'.[27]

In 1754 James Lloyd died, and his son, another James, carried on farming and later in 1758 purchased the manor of How Court.[28] During the years that followed a great deal of land in Lancing was purchased by James Lloyd and passed over to his son, James Martin Lloyd, *c.* 1785, some thirteen years before his own death in 1798. In 1827 the manor of 'North Lancing and Monks, South Lancing and Lyons' was conveyed by deed to James Martin Lloyd from John Biddulph. Nearly four-fifths of the parish of Lancing belonged to James Martin Lloyd after this purchase.

LLOYD FAMILY

ARMS:- PARTY PER BEND SINISTER, ERMINES AND ERMINE, A LION RAMPAMT OR.

Fig. 12.

Sir James Martin Lloyd died in 1844, having left to his daughter, Rebecca M. Lloyd, the estate which he had in Lancing manor. She died in 1846, and left her estate to her step-mother, Lady Lloyd. In the year 1858 Lady Lloyd herself died, having left her whole estates and interest in Lancing manor to Colonel Carr-Lloyd in her will. The Colonel's name had been Carr, and it was a provision of Lady Lloyd's will that, in order to hold that estate, he should take the name of Lloyd by royal license within one year of coming into possession of it. However, before the death of Lady Lloyd he had become Colonel Carr-Lloyd in March 1855.[29]

For nearly twenty years Colonel Carr-Lloyd was lord of the manor, but on Tuesday, 12 June 1877, he shot himself through the head and he died on Friday, 15 June. The reasons for his suicide are not readily apparent, but it may have been because of financial difficulties caused by the large expense of providing sea defences on his property.

His son, James Martin Carr-Lloyd, then became the new lord of the manor. During the latter part of the 19th and early part of the 20th centuries the manor was split up and sold. In 1896 two fields in How Court were exchanged with Lancing College for part of Malthouse farmland in Grinstead Lane. In 1907 Old Salts and New Salts were sold to the 'Shoreham and Lancing Land Company', and in 1920 the Manor House and its garden were bought by Lancing College from the executors of Carr-Lloyd. Later additional purchase was made of downland. The Manor House and garden were purchased by Worthing and District Rural Council in 1935, and were still in their possession when the house was demolished in 1972.

One of the more unusual privileges which the lords of the manor of Lancing enjoyed was the right of the wrecks,[30] a right often disputed by the superior lords of Bramber. Accord-

Fig. 13. Barque 'Ophir', Captain Olson, stranded off Lancing,
6 December 1896

ing to the historian Cartwright, the 'Hundred Rolls' state that 'William de Braose has wrecks of the sea against the Port of Shoreham', but also adds that 'John de Camoys, Nigel de Brok [Lord of Lancing] and others have wrecks of the sea against their lands, by ancient tenure, but those which are cast upon their lands and found must be kept a year and a day, and if any one can satisfactorily prove a property in them within that time, they shall be restored to him, all costs having first been paid'.

Another document, the 'Placeta Coronae' (7 Edward I), is quoted by Cartwright to show this ancient 'right of wrecks' as 'Concerning liberties the Jurors say, that John de Camoys, Nigel de Brok etc. claim to have wreck of the sea for their lands, but by what warrant they know not . . .' and '. . . John and Nigel come and say that they and their ancestors have used the aforesaid liberties before the conquest of England and beyond the memory of man'.

Besides the right of wrecks, the lord of the Manor of Lancing was also entitled to the best anchor and cable of every foreign ship and the best cable of every British ship which may be stranded or driven ashore. The Court Rolls of Lancing[31] contain many examples of this right. A few interesting extracts are as follows:

27 June 1677 (translated from Latin):

> A Court Baron of Dame Mary Goring, Mother and Guardian of Sir William Goring Baronet. A presentment of a little boat 'Anglice' a pinnace boat, which was cast upon the shore of the sea within the manor of Lancing and became a wreck, which said little boat was seized and sold by the Bailiff of the Lady for 3 shillings.

4 March 1678:

> A Court Baron presented by the Homage. Since the last court a cask of brandy containing 40 gallons was cast by the sea upon dry land.

29 November 1701 (at a Court Baron of Sir William Goring):

> We present a cable and anchor taken on the sea shore, about November last two years, which was appraised and sold by the Lord of this manor for £8 5s 0d as forfeited by the Lord for the ship striking this manor.

17 November 1702 (at a Court Baron of William Goring, Baronet):

> We present a mast taken up as wreck near the middle of Sir William Goring's marsh called the Sea Mills.

22nd September 1703 (at a Court Baron of William Goring, Baronet):

> We present a cable and anchor seized by the Lord of this manor about 30 rod west of the Harbour's mouth for a French ship striking and lying four tides at high water mark within the said manor.

In 1755 the right of wrecks was tried before Mr. Justice Wilmot. Mr. Biddulph (Lord of Lancing) was the plaintiff and parole evidence and court rolls were produced from the year 1663 in support of his case. Although two trials from the seventh year of Edward I's reign and one from the seventh year of Edward III were referred to by the defendant, judgment was given for the plaintiff. It thus appears that those ancient decisions were not conclusive evidence against the undisputed rights for 92 years (i.e., 1663–1755).

These undisputed rights continued for at least another 118 years. There is evidence of this in the court case of Lloyd *v.* Ingram in 1868, which involved a dispute regarding ownership of land south of the river Adur and to the east of the 'new' harbour mouth made in 1760. James Penfold was called as witness. He was 70 at the time of the trial, and occupied New Salts Farm. The transcript of the case states that he came to reside in Lancing in 1816 and became Land Steward to Sir James Lloyd in 1822. Eventually in 1827 he became reeve of the manor of Lancing, which meant he attended to the wrecks along the coast of the said manor.

The modern foreshore of Lancing is no longer owned by a lord of the manor. Any wrecks or cargo from wrecks washed up by the sea valued over £20 must be notified to the local Receiver of Wrecks via the coastguard office. Any such goods or parts of wreck taken without notifying the Receiver of Wrecks would be classified as stolen.

### The Manor of How (Hoe Court)

At the time of the Domesday Survey How is described as a Berewick (a severed or outlying portion) of the manor of Hurstpierpoint, held by William FitzBarnard from the Lord of Lewes, William de Warenne, while a knight also held one hide. In 1209 Nicholas, Bishop of Chichester, granted to the vicar of Henfield all the tithes 'arising from the lands and tenements of Broadville and How, near Lancing'.[32] Thus How was still divided in two parts, but both parts were now identified as Broadville and How.

*Broadville.*—In the Subsidy Lists for Lancing in 1296, 1327 and 1333 can be found the names Robro de Bordevyle, Johe Burdeville and Joho Bourdevyle respectively. This is a Norman name and it is quite possible that the knight mentioned in the Domesday Survey may also have been a Bordeville; there is no doubt that 'Broadville' is a corruption of the family name Bordeville. About 1247 Walter de Bordevile and Isabel, his wife, granted one acre of land in the parish of Lancing to Boxgrove Priory, and this was later confirmed by their son Robert.[33]

An interesting article relating to Itchingfield in Sussex[34] shows the gradual change of the Norman name:

| Date | Name |
|------|------|
| 1220 and 1237 | Bordeville |
| 1249 and 1280 | Birdeville |
| 1366 and 1422 | Burdevyle |
| 1418, 1479, 1483 | Bordevile |
| 1478 | Burdfield |
| 1507 | Boordvyle |
| 1544 | Burdfield |
| 1686 | Birdfield |

Another Robert Burdeville died seized of land in Lancing in 1377, held of Bramber honor, while a Thomas Burdeville of Etons in Ashurst had connections with land in Lancing in 1534.[35] There appears to be no further mention of the name Burdeville in connection with Lancing after this date, and apart from a certain John Hyde of 'Byrdvyles' in a deed of 1555,[36] the descent of Broadville is lost until 1608. At this date a survey of the manor of How Court was made[37] in which it was entered that Sir Edward Caryll made a claim for How Court, and his land adjacent to it was described as '. . . part of his freehold field called Broadfield . . .' in one copy of the survey, while

in another version '. . . part of his ffarme called Birvills . . .'
In an 'inquisition post mortem' of 1609[38] Edward Caryll
died seized of '. . . manor or farm of Birdvills in Westgrinstead,
Henfield and Launsing 30/- . . .', and again in 1616, Thomas
Caryll died seized of '. . . the manor of Birdfieldes . . .'[39]
The manor then descended with Washington[40] until *c.* 1664.
when Caryll Molyneux, Viscount Molyneux, grandson of Sir
Thomas Caryll was assessed of two hearths there.[41] It must have
passed later to Thomas Shadwell, for in 1729 he devised it to
his son Thomas. (The map of Lancing for 1770 shows Shadwell
Down adjacent to the How Court property and it was probably
the same person who owned Shadwell's Farm in Lancing and a
portion of marshland shown as 'Shadwell's Nimbles'.) In 1731
Hugh Roberts conveyed it to Thomas Luxford[42] although it
appears from agricultural memoranda written by James Lloyd
that Roberts remained as tenant at least until 1738.[43] In 1736
a deed shows the exchange of land between Mary Sheldon,
owner of How Court, and Thomas Luxford, the owner of Birvils
Farm, for the settling of bounds between the two farms.[44] In
1780 Mrs. Luxford was shown as the owner[45] and in 1796 it
passed to Mr. Willes, who within the year had settled it on his
son, William. In 1811 it was settled on William and Young
Willes[46] and in 1838 it was owned by John Willes, the cricketer
who introduced round-arm bowling into first-class cricket.

Mr. B. W. T. Handford in his book *Lancing: A History of
SS. Mary and Nicolas College, Lancing 1848-1930* supplies the
remainder of the story of Burfield's Farm, which had now
become known as Birvills Farm. Apparently John Willes mortgaged his property to a certain Anne Levett who foreclosed on
his death in 1852. An advertisement announcing the sale of
Birvills Farm in the same year described the property as 'rich
arable, meadow and pasture land part of which adjoins the High
Road. Beautifully undulated, commanding delightful prospects
of the sea and surrounding country and on which is growing
some thriving and ornamental plantation and stately timber'.
It was also indicated that it would be a suitable site for a
gentleman's mansion since it adjoined Lancing manor.

The farm contained about 177 acres and Nathaniel Woodard
bought this property together with Malthouse Farm from Anne

Levett in 1852 for £9,000. Lancing College was eventually built on this site and the farm is still in existence, but is known as the College farm.

During the 19th century How Court and Birvills Farm paid tithes of corn and hay from about 294 acres to the rector of West Grinstead, continuing its early connections with that parish, and also the tithes from about 45 acres to the vicar of Henfield. Grinstead Lane in Lancing commemorates the connection with West Grinstead.

*Howcourt.*—In 1242 Richard le Large held two fees in Howcourt and at West Grinstead of Bramber honor in 1242.[47] It is possible that William le Large, who held land in Lancing at the end of the 12th century, may have been a previous owner.[48] In 1276 William de Braose granted to John of Coombes 49 acres at How.[49]

The neighbouring parishes of Applesham and Coombes were held by William FitzNorman at the time of Domesday and later by Hugh Norman de Combe. This family later became the 'de Combes' of which John de Combes was undoubtedly a descendant. In 1279 there is an account of a trial between William de Stainis and Alice, his wife, plaintiffs, and John de Combe, defendant, respecting his right to 40 acres of arable and 12 shillings rent in How.[50] The Subsidy Lists for Lancing show, in 1327, Rico de Applesham and, in 1332, Rico de Combes (no doubt the same person). In an 'inquisition post mortem' of 1351 it appears that Richard de Combes (the same person as shown above, or his son) died seized of certain tenements at How, in the Parish of Lancing, worth £1 6s. 8d. per annum, and held in demesne of John de Mowbray, by the service of an eighth part of a knight's fee, and a rent of 5d. to be paid on St. Thomas's Day.[51] The manor descended with Coombes until 1453, and later Ralph Shirley of Wiston apparently bought Howcourt from an unknown vendor.[52] It then descended with Buddington in Wiston until 1551, when Francis Shirley conveyed it to Edward Fynes, Lord Clinton,[53] although at the same time an indenture was made between John Grevett and Francis Shirley[37] of the demesne land of Howcourt. Later in 1578 Francis died seized of messuages, etc., in Lancing[54] and in 1592 his son Thomas was apparently the lessee of Howcourt.[55]

Lord Clinton had conveyed the manor to the Crown by 1578 and in 1608 a survey was made by Thomas Marshall, Surveyor of the King's possessions,[37] by virtue of a commission directed by the oaths of Thomas Whatman and '19 other honest men'. From these documents, of which there were three variations of the survey, and from later information it is possible to describe the property which was the demesne land of the manor. Howcourt had a Mansion House, two barns, stable, and a dovehouse. These were almost certainly on the site of the present Hoecourt barns and cottages. Adjoining the house was pasture land of 15 acres called the Upper Laine. Next to this was 15 acres of arable land called the Middle Laine, 10 acres of which belonged to Burvills farm. Another parcel of land, approximately 16 acres, was known as the Netherlaine. This presumably was the field known later as the '16 acre field' near the College. Other land mentioned was a close of arable land known as the 'Waterpoole piece' (as yet the location of this field is unidentified), and the 'Deane' of approximately four acres. Two pieces of marshland were mentioned which totalled seven acres, these almost certainly being the Ladywell brooks. With this land, totalling about 67 acres, went the common of pasture for 150 sheep on the Downs.

It was assumed by the historian Cartwright that from 1608 Howcourt belonged to the Caryll family and descended through that family until the property was sequestrated in 1750 and then bought by Sir Merrick Burrell. This, however, is incorrect, for in 1629 the manor was granted at fee farm to Sir Allan Apsley,[56] and his son Peter sold it in 1633 to Henry Bartelot of Stopham in Sussex, when Howcourt was described as part of the exchange lands of Edward Clinton, late in the tenure of John Gravet.[57] In 1641 it was placed in trust for Francis Watker of Pulborough,[58] but was sold to Richard Mille of Stopham in 1656 in order to pay Francis Watker's debts.[59] In 1659 the manor was purchased by Thomas Smith and Edward Goringe, executors of the will of Margaret Dobel, and then settled on her grandchildren, Judith and Margaret Rose.[60] In 1681 Margaret's husband, Sir Joseph Sheldon, died, and his will named his brother, Daniel Sheldon, to inherit Howcourt.[61]

Daniel died in 1699 seized of the manor and was succeeded by his daughters, Judith and Mary, as co-heirs.[62] Judith died in 1725 and left her estate to Mary[35] and later in 1731 she leased the demesne lands to James Lloyd.[63] In 1737 the the property was mortgaged to Samuel Levinge of the Inner Temple, London[64] and after Mary's death, *c.* 1739, Howcourt passed to him.

After Samuel Levinge's death in 1747 the property was left to his cousin, Elizabeth Levinge,[65] who married Delme Vanleythyson of Oulton in Suffolk, and then settled it on Thomas Pelham in 1751.[66] In 1758 Thomas Pelham sold it to James Lloyd[67] whose father (who died in 1754) had leased the demesne land from 1731. Howcourt (now spelt Hoecourt) remained in the Lloyd family until the death of James Martin Carr-Lloyd in 1919. The estate was then split up and sold during the years 1920–28. In 1975 the farms at Hoe Court and the College farms (originally Birvills) were being jointly farmed.

There have been several references to the old house at Hoe Court, but no description or plan of the building has been found. Its true site is not known, as it disappeared in the early part of the 18th century, but is believed to be on, or very near, the site of the present Hoecourt cottages. The origin of the name 'Howcourt' is somewhat obscure. Mawer and Stenton[68] state that How is from 'hoh', on a spur of land, whereas another meaning has been taken as 'high ground'. The 'court' may refer either to the fact that the manor court was held in the house or that the buildings actually form a courtyard.

*The Manor of St. John's*

The earliest record of this small manor in Lancing is in a court case of 1591[69] when Walter Gybbons, clerk mentions '. . . a Manor of St. John's lying in Launsinge whose rentes amount to XVII shillings a year' and '. . . The Queen Majestie hath a manor in Launsinge called by the name of St. John's and there be freeholders and copyholders belonging thereto. There is about XVII or XVIII shillings yearlie rent payable to the same manor and that William Hyde and one Gentes widow tenaunts to St. John have some land in Howe Field'.

The documents also mention '. . . Ye Highe Waye leading thorowe Lansiunge aforesaid unto ye ferrye called St John ferrye etc.'. The 'Highe Waye' was the road which ran from the manor to the *Sussex Pad* inn. Before the bridge was built across the River Adur in 1784 there existed a ferry (see map of Lancing marshes), and no doubt it was this ferry which was once called the 'St. John Ferrye'. It was quite probable that the *Sussex Pad* was connected with the ferry as there have been indications that the old *Sussex Pad* (burnt down in 1905) was probably built before 1591.[70]

In 1316 William Paynell granted the ferry together with his manor of Cokeham and 32 acres of land in Lancing to the prior and canons of Herryngham (Hardham, near Pulborough) on account of their poverty. At Cokeham there was a 'hospital' appropriated to the Priory of St. John of Jerusalem, whilst in Shoreham there was also a Priory of the same order which was washed away by the sea in the 15th century. No doubt monks travelled from one Priory to the other via the ferry, hence the name 'St. John's Ferry'. A further connection with the Shoreham priory and St. John's of Lancing is a piece of land known as St. John's Wall in St. John's Road, Shoreham, which was part of the manor of Lancing. When the monasteries were suppressed by Henry VIII the manor of St. John's must have reverted to the Crown and hence the reason for the manor belonging to 'The Queen Majestie' (Elizabeth I) in 1591.

Two later inquisitions give us more information about the manor. They refer to Henry Goringe, a knight, who died in 1594 while in possession of 'land in Lancing called Smythes Longe Gardeine and Coldens held of the manor of St. John's, 13s 4d . . .',[71] and William Goringe, who died in 1601, having in his possession 'parcels of land in Launcinge called Smithes Longe Garden and Cobdayes held of Queen of Manor of St John's, 13s 4d'.[72]

It appears from these inquisitions and other deeds[73] that the manor consisted of scattered pieces of land in North Lancing, part of which was known as 'Smiths Long Garden'. The position of the 'Long Garden' has not been located, but deeds showing descendants of the Hyde family in 1646 mention certain pieces of land which still seem to indicate a connection with the manor of St. John's. The names of these pieces are: The Wealmershe, containing one and a half acres adjoining Shoreham Haven; one acre in the Wealefield; one acre in the Sladefield; and four and a half acres in the How Laynes in East Furlong. The last item in particular confirms the earlier reference of 1591 concerning 'land in Howe Field'. All these pieces of land lie around the *Sussex Pad* and the causeway or ferry.

A later deed of 1689-90 connects John Hide of Worthing with Long Garden in North Lancing. From this point the descent of the garden can be traced through William Rowland and the Lindupp family of Worthing until 1786 when the land was purchased by James Martin Lloyd. The lands were then amalgamated into J. M. Lloyd's large estate, and the name of Long Garden does not reappear.

*The Manor of Lyons*

This manor, although not in the parish of Lancing, became connected with Lancing in the 16th century. It undoubtedly took its name from Henry de Lyons, a knight, who held land in Broadwater in 1296.[74]

Several offices were held by Henry de Lyons during his lifetime. He was elected as Magistrate for the county of Sussex in September 1279 and was acting in the Chichester, Arundel and Bramber Rapes from September 1279 to May 1288. In 1292 he was a Guildford Gaol Delivery Justice, and in 1297 was summoned for military service. He held land in Chichester, Arundel, Bramber and Pevensey Rapes.[75]

Due to the lack of information on Lyons of Broadwater, a strip of land in Compton, Sussex, recorded as held by Henry de Lyons, has been used to trace the remaining history of the family.[76] In 1316 Compton was held by Richard de Lyons and later, in 1329 by the heirs of Richard. A John de Lyons is recorded in 1336, 1347 amd 1349, but there is no further mention after this date. It has been suggested that the family was wiped out by the Black Death and the holdings reverted to the overlord. In the case of Lyons of Broadwater it would then descend as Broadwater did, through the families of the Camoys and Radmylds.

The next positive identification of Lyons occurs in 1543-4, when the manors of Lyons and Wyke and tenements in Magna-Brodewater, Parva Brodewater, Shipley, Wiston, Launcying, Sountyng, Sele, and Stenyng were quitclaimed to William Goring, knight. Thus it descended through the families of Goring and Biddulph as did the manor of Lancing. Lyons, being a neighbouring manor held by the same lord of the manor, became incorporated in the title of Lancing as 'The Manor of North Lancing and Monks, South Lancing and Lyons'. Eventually the manor of Lyons became known as Lyons Farm as can be seen from an advertisement which appeared in the *Sussex Advertiser* on Monday, 11 June 1770:

> To be let or sold and entered upon at Michaelmas 1771, or sooner if required, a Farm in Broadwater and Sompting called Lyons Farm in the occupation of John Penfold, about 240 acres, the housing and land in good order one mile from the sea, 5 from Steyning and 10 from Brighthelmstone.

A series of later deeds relating to the farm show that in 1879 it consisted of 313 acres and a settlement was made in contemplation of marriage between Blanche Ellen Crofts and Samuel Barrington Tristram.[77] Later in 1923 Blanche Ellen Tristram and others sold the farm to Gordon Charles Lucas. The farm then descended as follows:

6 July 1934. Gordon Charles Lucas to E. G. Annis.

25 February 1935. Ernest George Annis to E. N. C. Annis.

25 December 1938. E. N. C. Annis died and left Lyons to his wife, V. R. Annis.

14 April 1939. V. R. Annis to E. C. F. Sawyer and T. H. Sawyer.

12 October 1956. E. C. F. and T. H. Sawyer sold the farmhouse and a small area of ground to Worthing Corporation.

The farmhouse no longer exists, but a small area of original farmland now known as 'Lyons Farm recreation ground' remains and is maintained by Worthing Borough Council.

## Ancient Port of Pende (Woods Manor)

Although not originally identified as a manor of Lancing, Pende had definite connections with the parish. Ancient Pende has been located as being between Bramber, Shoreham, and Lancing. From the available references, its site has been placed as south-west of New Salts Farm, lying at a place now beneath the sea. It was known to be a port between 1250 and 1420 with recognised port officials.[78]

There is no mention of Pende in the Domesday Book, but *c.* 1250 there is mention of a Sele charter of a Ralf Coppenden of Pende[79] and the Subsidy Lists of Lancing for 1327 and 1332[80] show a William Coppenden, no doubt a descendant of Ralf. In 1324 a Thomas de Hurst sold land in South Lancing, North Lancing and Pende.[81] Later from surviving wool accounts of Sussex in Richard II's reign[82] we find that on 3 January 1379 a Thomas Hanepere was master of the ship *Margaret of Pende,* and again the Subsidy Lists of 1332[83] show a William Haneper as an inhabitant of Lancing.

In 1351 there is a mention of sea walls at 'La Pende' between Bramber, Shoreham and Lancing.[79] Dugdale's *History of Imbanking and Draining* mentions that in 1359 a commission was set up to repair some sea walls at a place called Pende[84] (described as being in the same position as in 1351), which had been damaged by inundations and ravages of the French and Spanish. The last two references are particularly interesting because a recent comparison of two old maps of the salt-marshes of Lancing locates Pende more precisely. One of these maps, undated, but estimated to be *c.* 1590,[85] shows 'the owld wales in the sea' (*wales* were timber sea defences) at the estimated site of Pende. The other map, dated 1622,[86] has an even more interesting note in approximately the same position, namely: 'In this place beinge a myle distante from the shore in the sea are owld wales to be [? seen] at lower water [? which] ar commonly called axaparte', and in the middle of the words are drawings of four walls. Both of these references must surely signify the same place!

The word Pende is probably derived from the Old English *pynd*, meaning enclosure and possibly describes the old partially enclosed harbour. Further mentions of Pende occur in 1378 and 1379 when John Poughe was master of a ship named *Goodyer of Pende.*[82] In 1371 a certain Simon of Lancing was made a 'Searcher' in Pende[79] and Henry Cheal, in his book,

*The Story of Shoreham,* mentions that a ship sailed in 1420 from Pende-juxta-Shoreham to Rouen, carrying provisions, as did many others employed in the same service.

In 1587 on the map prepared for the defence against the Armada[87] there is a water channel shown flowing westwards from the river at Shoreham, terminating in a lagoon marked 'Penhowse', in approximately the position of the modern Shopsdam Road Area. Penhowse is immediately south-east of the area once known as Penhill, which is almost certainly derived from Pende-hill, the hill overlooking the port of Pende.

It has been suggested that Penhouse is therefore connected with Pende and is probably the remains of the port of Pende, which declined as the mouth of the river moved eastwards, due to the gradual movement of the shingle beach. However, there is another theory which says that the river Arun once had its outlet into the sea at the same place as the river Adur. We find the first mention of this when, in 1929, Joseph Fowler issued the book *The High Stream of Arundel* after he had discovered the Water Bailiff's Book of 1638. In the Water Bailiff's Book it was recorded that in 1638 there was 'an old tradition' that 'the High Stream in Arundel Levell did Issue in former times into the sea at Pen-house in Lancing, where Bramber river then likewise vented itself'.

In his *Waters of Arun* the late Hadrian Allcroft also came to this conclusion after a long investigation. The 1587 map shows a series of lagoons, landing stages and beacons along the beach between Penhouse and Ferring. It was these lagoons that Allcroft says were the successive outlets of the Arun as the river-mouth moved westwards over a long period of time. If this theory is correct, then by 1250 (when the port of Pende was known to have been in existence) the mouth of the Arun must have receded to the west of Shopsdam Road area and left a convenient stretch of water which formed the port of Pende.

The western end of the lagoon marked 'Penhowse' on the map of 1587 lies at a spot now known as Shopsdam Road, which in the 17th and 18th centuries was 'Lancing Shoppsdam' or 'the damm'. This was a dam which led across the water channel to the 'shopps' on the beach. These shops were fishermen's huts used for dealing with their catch.

The 'beating of the bounds' of the manor of North Lancing and Monks, South Lancing and Lyons[88] show in every instance that when reaching the Lancing shops at low watermark on the beach a turn northwards is made and the party walked round the shops back to low watermark on the other side. In 1711 the land which contained the shops and caused the detour of the party was known as Woods Manor and was not part of the larger manors of North and South Lancing (see map of Area No. 4). However, the historian Cartwright mentions that in 1609 it was known as the 'manor of Lancing' and belonged to the Crown. If Allcroft and the ancient tradition are correct, then this small manor corresponds exactly to where the two rivers once emptied into the sea and would therefore be the later entrance to the port of Pende.

In 1608 a reference in Maskell's manuscript Survey of Sussex[89] states 'that the tenants of this manor [Lancing] do and of right may intercommon with their cattle with the tenants of Sir Henry Goring (Kt) on a parcell of waste or common called Launceing Have [Lancing Haven]'.

Woods Manor was owned by the Crown in 1609-22. The references to this manor are very few and far between and nothing like a complete record has been obtained. The exact size of the manor is not known, but is probably somewhere in the region of five acres. The name 'Woods Manor' came into being around 1700 when it was obtained by John Wood (whether by purchase or inheritance is not known). later in 1722 it passed to Eleanor Wood.

In the court case Lloyd *v.* Ingram 1868 Woods Manor was referred to several times, and although by then it had changed hands a number of times this name seems to have been retained. In 1776 it was sold to James Martin Lloyd and was thus absorbed into his Lancing estate.

The following list shows some of the owners of the manor.

| Date | Name |
| --- | --- |
| 1609–1622 | Vested in the Crown |
| 1629 | –. Raynes |
| 1701–1721 | John Wood (it was known as Woods Manor during this period, but whether John Wood was owner throughout is not known) |

*continued*

*continued*

| Date | Name |
|---|---|
| 1722 | Eleanor Wood |
| 1732 | John Fowler, Esq. |
| 1755 | (sold to) Mr. Brown |
| 1756–1762 | Mr. Poole |
| 1776 | Mr. J. M. Lloyd (from this point the piece of land in question loses its identity and becomes part of Mr. Lloyd's large estate) |

During the 16th and 17th centuries there are several instances of names which have prefix Pen, possibly still retaining the link with the old Pende, e.g., Penbush Furlong, Penhill Laine, Pen Garden, all of which were situated around the site of the more modern Penhill. The ground at Penhill is higher in relation to its surroundings and if, in fact, Penhill was originally Pendehill then it may be this land which was sold in 1324.

Today the only connection with the ancient Pende is retained in the name of Penhill Road which is in the vicinity of the old site.

*Church Farm (North Farm)*

The site of the old farmhouse and outbuildings is opposite North Lancing church. Although the farm was earlier known as North Farm, during the 19th century it was often referred to as Church Farm.

There are very few early references to North Farm, but it seems certain that this was the original centre of the manor of North Lancing. In the 18th century the concentration of land belonging to North Farm, which was owned by the lord of the manor of Lancing (Charles Biddulph) on the north and south of the farm, indicates the gradual clearing of land for agricultural purposes. If North Farm was previously known as North Lancing Farm, and was like many other manors which eventually became farms, it would originally have been North Lancing Manor (or as it was often referred to 'the Manor of Lancing alias North Lancing'). The descent of this farm then reads as the Manor of North Lancing and would account for the lack of early references to North Farm.

It seems quite feasible that this was the site of the original Saxon settlement at Lancing, and the fact that the church was

was situated opposite the farm early in the 12th century seems to confirm this.

By 1770 the farmland amounted to 202 acres. In 1838 it was 164 acres. The earliest known buildings on the farm consisted of a farmhouse with a coach-house to the north and barns and cottages directly opposite the church. A garden was situated to the south of the farmhouse, and a large field at the rear of North Farm was called Cart house (horse?) field in 1770 and the Grove in 1838. The farmhouse still exists, but was nearly demolished when Church Close was formed. It is now divided into two houses and still retains a small but interesting cellar at the front of the house. The cottages and barn disappeared when Fircroft Avenue was formed in the 1930s.

The following list shows the known owners and occupiers.

| Date | Owners | Occupier/Renter | Name of Farm |
|------|--------|-----------------|--------------|
| 1770 | Biddulph family | Mr. Graves | North Farm |
| 1780–84 | Biddulph family | Richard Jay | North Farm |
| 1785-1822 | Biddulph family | Thomas Lidbetter | North Farm |
| 1822–27 | Biddulph family | Thomas Lidbetter | North/Church Farm |
| 1828–58 | Lloyd family | Thomas/George Bushby | North Farm |
| 1903–12 | Lloyd family | Mrs. Wellington | Church Farm House |

## Brickhouse Farm (Newman's Farm)

The site of the old farmhouse and outbuildings of Brickhouse Farm is in North Lancing on the south side of the Manor Road between the car park of the *Sussex Potter* (formerly the Corner House) and the churchyard. The house, at present named 'Friars Acre', stands adjacent to the east side of the path which leads to the vicarage. It is brick-built, timber-framed, and dated 1659, and no doubt this is the original 'Brickhouse' mentioned in a deed of 1679–80 when some marshland belonging to the farm was sold.[90]

At that time John Streater was owner of the farm, which contained approximately 54 acres. The next mention of the farm occurs in another deed, dated 20 March 1735, when we are informed that the farm contains 41 acres (13 acres of

Fig. 14. 'Friar's Acre', North Lancing (formerly 'Brickhouse Farm'; Chapter Four, No. 50).

marshland were previously sold) and comprises 'a messuage, 2 barns, a stable, granary and other buildings called Brickhouse in Lancing'.[91]

In 1734 the farm was owned by Robert Leeves of Steyning and was for the use of him and his heirs until the solemnisation of an intended marriage between Henry Johnson of Bramber, a maltster, and Hester Leeves, second daughter of Robert Leeves. After the marriage it was for the use of Robert Leeves for life and then the heirs of Hester. The marriage took place soon afterwards, and later Robert Leeves died intestate. Hester Leeves survived her father and had one son and four daughters. She died, however, before her husband. It appears that the son then owned the farm, for in 1799 the owner was Henry Johnson of Waldron, Sussex, a tanner by trade, who had a wife Elizabeth.[92]

Between 1799 and 1800 the farm was sold to James Newman, a yeoman,[93] and from this point on was known as Newman's Farm. From 1912 (and probably before that) the house was known as Newman's Farmhouse. This name continued until about 1936 when a new owner changed it to 'Red Oak Manor'. This name in turn continued until it was changed to 'Friar's Acre' (the present name) at some date between 1949 and 1953.[94]

Prior to the Divison and Enclosure act the land belonging to Brickhouse Farm was in scattered pieces throughout the parish The names which follow show some of the furlongs and fields incorporating land belonging to the farm (many of the furlongs can be identified by referring to the maps): Withy Tree Marsh, Carter's Park, Brook Furlong, Eelspring Furlong, Crutch Furlong, Longlands Furlong, Capenham, Northover, Penn Gardens, Short Butts, The Greenhurst, Callice field, adjoining to Barrowhole field, Stony Bottom Furlong, Hampshire Furlong, East Furlong, in Upper West Lane, East Lane Furlong.

After enclosures were carried out in Lancing, James Newman was awarded the area south of the farmhouse down to Crabtree Lane in the south, bordered on the west by West Lane and partly on the east by Church Path (now First Avenue), and on the north-east by the part of the Manor Road which runs by the side of the Manor Grounds. (This road was formed between 1803 and 1805 when J. M. Lloyd set out his private grounds, now the Manor recreation ground. The area of this farmland was described as being situated in the furlongs called Longlands, Stony Bottom and part of the Links (see map of Area No. 1). The remainder of the land was Newman's Brook and Withy Tree Marsh (see map of Area No. 3).

By 1812 it appears that James Newman had died, for in that year Mrs. Newman is shown as owner-occupier of the farm.[95] In 1822 the farm passed to J. M. Lloyd, probably by purchase, and later became part of North Farm (or Church Farm as it was often called).

A summary follows of the known owners and occupiers of the farm and later the farmhouse:

| Date | Owners | Occupier/Renter |
|---|---|---|
| 1679 | John Streater | (Probably John Streater) |
| 1734–1736 | Leeves family | |
| 1736–1799 | Johnson family | From 1780 James Newman |
| 1800–1822 | Newman family | From 1812 Mrs. Newman |
| 1822–1838 | J. M. Lloyd | Thomas Bushby (part of North Farm) |

| Farmhouse | Occupier | Name of House |
|-----------|----------|---------------|
| 1912–1936 | C. D. Gooderham | Newman's Farmhouse |
| 1936–1949 | E. J. Shadwick | Red Oak Manor |
| 1953 | Mrs. N. Smith | 'Friar's Acre' (present name) |

*Edwards of John Swift. 1657 b. 2/3/1657*

## Culverhouse Farm

The site of the farmhouse and outbuildings is in North Road, almost opposite the old almshouses. An old flint wall which once stood in front of the house was demolished together with all the other buildings and the site is now occupied by a row of shops which commence at Culver Road (named after the old farm) and stretch southwards.

A note referring to the derivation of the word 'Culver' appears in the Sussex Archaeological Collections.[96] It shows that the word comes from the Anglo-Saxon *culfre, culefere,* a dove or pigeon, and that Sussex abounds in Culver-houses, Culver-crofts and Culver-fields. This is confirmed in the 1805 Inclosure Award and the 1838 Tithe Map of Lancing where a field at the rear of Culver House is named 'Dove-house close' and 'Pigeon house field' respectively.

One of the first references to Culverhouse Farm in Lancing appears in 1706 when a copy of the Court Rolls of the Manor of North Lancing and Monks, South Lancing and Lyons, shows the admission of Francis Langford, aged nine years, son of Anne Langford, to the copyhold premises called Culverhouse, containing 24 acres. It is almost certain that the farm existed before 1706, but as yet no earlier references have been found. No doubt the missing Court Rolls of Lancing would contain this information.

By 1739 the farm was owned by J. Lloyd for a deed in the author's possession shows a lease for one year to a Mr. Swift by J. Lloyd. The 1770 map of Lancing also shows the farm to be owned by J. Lloyd, and later in 1838 the Tithe Award for Lancing shows that it was still owned by a member of the Lloyd family.

The following list shows the known owners and occupiers:

| Date | Owner | Occupier |
|------|-------|----------|
| 1706 | Francis Langford | |
| 1739 | J. Lloyd | Mr. Swift. |
| 1770 | J. Lloyd | |
| 1838 | J. M. Lloyd | James Penfold, snr. and jnr. |
| 1874 | | Mrs. Penfold. |
| 1876–1895 | | Mr. C. Duke |
| 1905–1912 | | James Cass |

*Yew Tree Farm*

The name 'Yew Tree Farm' first appears on the 1869 Ordnance Survey map of Lancing (six inches to the mile). Goring House, at the junction of South Street and Penhill Road, stands on the site of the old farmhouse. Penhill Road runs through the middle of the site of the old farm outbuildings and yard adjoining the farmhouse as shown on the Tithe Map of Lancing for 1838. It is most probable that Goring House was the old farmhouse, for the particulars and conditions of sale of the farm of November 1790[97] show that the premises were copyhold and held of the Manor of North Lancing and Monks, South Lancing and Lyons, and mention a '. . . well built Farmhouse (lately fitted up and used as, and for a Lodging House, for the reception of company resorting to the seaside) . . .'. The site of Goring House is absolutely identical to the site of the farmhouse shown on the 1838 Tithe Map and of similar size. The appearance of the house suggests that it could be as old as 1790 and it is large enough to have been used as a lodging-house.

The name 'Yew Tree Farm' probably originated from either Yew Tree Cottages, or the yew tree outside the cottages, both of which were opposite the farm. The earlier names of this farm were Skinners, Grasmans, and Lees. The farm and its surrounding area are shown as Skinner's Copyhold on the enclosure map of Lancing in 1803, and in 1524–5 'John Skynner' and 'John a Lee hys servant' are shown as inhabitants of Lancing.[98] Another list of Lancing inhabitants in 1641 show further members of the Skinner family.[99]

In 1739–40 Charles Hersee was occupier of the farm. Later, in 1764, it was Israel Pain. In 1765 Mary Pain, only child and next heir to Israel, became the new owner, but Sarah Pain was appointed as guardian to Mary who was only 14 years old.

The land tax records show Mrs. Sarah Pain as owner in 1780, with J. Heather as the farmer. In 1786 the farm appears to have been obtained by J. Newman and remained in his family until 1790. In November 1790 the farm was sold by auction at the *Star* inn, New Shoreham, and was acquired by William Dabbs, whose family came from Oving. The farm was described in the brochure as having a farmhouse 'together with a Barn, Hovel, Strawyard, Garden Orchard and about 38 acres and a half of rich arable and pasture land . . .'. The Dabbs family still retained ownership of the farm in 1838. A William Dabbs, probably a son of the original owner, was responsible for having the original *Farmer's* inn built (now rebuilt and renamed the *Farmer's* hotel) in the early 1850s.

By the time the revised Ordnance Survey map was issued in 1899, Penhill Road had been formed and most of the farm outbuildings no longer existed. Only the farmhouse remained which was later known as Goring House (probably to commemorate the old link between Lancing and the Goring family). At the present time this house belongs to West Sussex County Council.

## Farms which Disappeared after the Enclosure Act of 1803

There were several farms in Lancing which lost their identity after enclosures were carried out there between 1803–5. There were others, too, which cannot be easily traced due to the names changing with successive owners and finally being amalgamated into larger estates. The sparse records which exist of these farms make their descent difficult to trace, but what follows are the known facts relating to the various farms.

### Grant's Farm

This was originally a small manor in North Lancing of approximately twenty acres which derived its name, the 'manor of Grauntes', from the Le Graunt family. The twenty acres were made up of mainly one-acre and half-acre strips scattered throughout the North Lancing fields, with one portion of a piece of marsh known as the Broad Dam brook. a *terrier* (survey) of Grant's Farm made in 1722,[99a] informs us that there was a farmhouse with an adjoining close, one orchard and a garden, one barn, a stable and a brewhouse. The actual site of the farmhouse has not, as yet, been located, but was possibly one of the buildings which were demolished when Lancing Manor grounds were formed around 1803-6.

The earliest record of the Graunt family which has so far come to light is in 1200 A.D., when Emma, widow of William le Graunt, dower in two hides and a half in Lancing petitioned William of Lancing.[99b] Her grandson, William Graunt, son of Robert le Graunt, son of William, was under age, and the land was held in custody by William of Lancing. Hence the grandfather of William would have been born *c.* 1140 A.D. A later document[100] shows: 'In Trinity term 1309, Alicia the widow of John le Graunt of Henfield brought an action against David the Chaplain of Steyning, for the third of a messuage, and twenty acres of land in Lancing, but on David's shewing that the same lands were demised to him by John, the son of Robert le Graunt, to hold for his life, and that Nicholas, the son of John was within age, and his body and lands in the custody of the Bishop of Chichester, her plea was not allowed'.

There is an earlier mention, in 1253, of a Richard le Graunt and his wife, purchasing land in New Shoreham, which later is mentioned as being part of Grant's Manor.

In 1399 a John Graunt lived in Lancing,[101] no doubt preserving the family's interest in the property, and more than a hundred years later in 1516 a post mortem inquisition mentions a very unfortunate member of the Graunt family; 'Peter Graunt is and has been from birth an idiot, seized of Graunt's manor in Launsyng'.[102]

The Lancing Parish Register shows that in 1568 John Graunt was buried in North Lancing churchyard. In 1567 he had married Annes, and their daughter, Alice, was buried in 1572. Annes, widow of John Graunt, married in 1571 one John Gente, junior. Presumably on the death of John Graunt in 1568 the manor was sold, because this is the last mention of the Graunt family in connection with the manor. In 1568

Stephen Bord of Cuckfield holds the Manor from Henry Goring, lord of the manor of North Lancing.[103] The manor descended through the Bord family until 1623 when there was a Deed of Feoffment by Herbert Bord of Lindfield to Henry Chatfield of Lancing, a yeoman, 'of the manor and lands called Grauntes . . .'.[104]

In 1669 Henry Chatfield sold the manor together with other land to Edward Jones, junior, a yeoman, for £306.[105] At some time during the next 10 years it appears that Grants first loses its title as a manor (although it appears again later), for Edward Jones' will of 1679 shows that he left '. . . to his daughter Frances the farm of Grants'. Frances herself married later, for her own will of 1732 describes her as 'Frances Young (late Frances Jones) of Launcing, widow', and shows that she left 'a messuage and lands called Grants Farm' to her nephew, John Langford of Lewes. The farm remained in the Langford family until 1780 when Charles Langford sold it to John Borrer.[106] By 1783 a William Borrer of Hurstpierpoint owned the property[107] and by 1795 had leased it to John Ford, maltster, of Lancing. Mr. Borrer built up a large estate in Lancing, and in 1796 the whole estate was exchanged with a farm called Nutknowle in Woodmancote, Sussex, belonging to James Lloyd of Lancing.[108]

Mr. Borrer's estate comprised four farms, namely: Malthouse farm, containing 110 acres; Northbarns farm, containing 24 acres; Floods farm, containing 23 acres; and Grants farm, containing 18¾ acres; totalling 175¾ acres.

The accounts for the transaction were as follows:[109]

|                                         | £      | s. | d. |
|-----------------------------------------|--------|----|----|
| Mr. Borrer's estate  ..    ..    ..   .. | 6,000  | 0  | 0  |
| Mr. Lloyd's estate   ..    ..    ..   .. | 3,550  | 0  | 0  |
|                                         | £2,450 | 0  | 0  |
| Minus Mr. Lloyd's timber ..   ..   .. | 730    | 18 | 7  |
|                                         | £1,719 | 1  | 5  |
| Plus Mr. Borrer's timber  ..   ..   .. | 55     | 0  | 0  |
|                                         | £1,774 | 1  | 5  |
| Mr. Lloyd paid Mr. Borrer ..  ..   .. | 1,800  | 0  | 0  |
|                                         | £25    | 18 | 7  |

Mr. Lloyd was building up a vast estate in Lancing and when the terms of the Enclosure Act were finally implemented in Lancing by 1805, all the farms mentioned were amalgamated into one estate and thus they lost their separate identities. Grant's Manor, or Farm, as it eventually became, had thus lasted for a period of at least 778 years, and, although small, certainly deserves its place in Lancing's history.

## Northbarns Farm

The first identifiable mention of Northbarns Farm is in 1648, when Sir William Goring and Henry Goring sold it to Richard Streater of Broadwater, a yeoman.[110] It appears that a tenant farmer, Thomas Easton, was in occupation, and sometime before this date it had been demised to William Blackman. (The Blackmans were an old Lancing family, and a portion of land in South Lancing was known as 'Blackman's Breach' for more than two hundred and fifty years.) The extent of the farm was originally 60 acres of land and marsh, and from a survey of 1722[111] there appears to have been no farmhouse, but only two barns, a close and a granary. There is no evidence to suggest that this farm had any connections with the Northbarns which exist at present. The barns and granary were most probably in North Lancing village, hence the name Northbarns.

In 1667 John Streater, son of Richard Streater, sold the farm to Edward Jones, senior, a yeoman,[112] who in turn assigned it to Edward Jones, junior, in 1672, by way of settlement in consideration of an intended marriage between the latter and Ann Turner.[113] The survey of 1722 shows the farm to contain 57½ acres, and by 1729, when Edward Jones's daughter Frances owned the farm it had only 24 acres.[114] From this point the farm appears to have descended the same way as Grant's Farm until it became part of Mr. Lloyd's estate in 1796.

## Malthouse Farm

This farm was by far the biggest of the group of four so far mentioned. It contained 110 acres and one house, three barns, and four closes. There were several farms in the Worthing,

Sompting, Lancing area known as the Malthouse, and it appears that this particular one is not connected with another of the same name which existed on the Upper Brighton Road, east of the Manor House.

This particular Malthouse Farm was owned by James Lloyd in 1796 and apparently was not resold. In 1803 the more modern Malthouse Farm was owned by a certain John Willes.[115]

The first mention of the farm by name is in 1722 when a *terrier* shows it to be occupied by Samuel Longley and containing 110 acres.[116] In 1729, Frances Young, daughter of Edward Jones, owned the farm together with the Northbarns, Flood's and Grant's Farms.[114] It then descended in the same way as Grant's Farm and ended up in Mr. Lloyd's estate in 1796.

### Flood's Farm

This farm was named after Thomas Flood of Broadwater, who owned it sometime before 1641.[117] No doubt it existed earlier, possibly under another name, but, as yet, cannot be traced.

The farm consisted of 22 acres of land and marsh scattered throughout Lancing. A farm survey of 1722 shows that the farmhouse was called or known by the sign of a ship.[118] The Overseer's records of Lancing confirm this when they refer to a Mr. Taylor's house known as 'The Ship', in 1795. Unfortunately, this name disappeared a few years later and many changes of tenancy have made the house virtually impossible to trace.

In 1641 the farm was sold by Sir William and Henry Goring to Judith Flood, sole daughter of Thomas Flood, for £200.[117] In 1652 Judith was the wife of a Thomas Heyward of Betchworth, Surrey. In 1658 Thomas and Judith sold the farm to 'Edward Jones *alias* Jerome of Lancing, a berebrewer'.[119] It was then assigned to Edward Jones, junior, as was Northbarns Farm, by way of settlement in consideration of an intended marriage between Edward Jones, junior, and Ann Turner. The farm then descended in the same way as Northbarns Farm until it was amalgamated into James Lloyd's estate in 1796.

The following list shows clearly the descent of the four farms:

### Grant's

| | | | |
|---|---|---|---|
| 1200 | William le Graunt | 1679 | Frances Jones |
| 1309 | David, chaplain of Steyning | 1729 | Frances Young (*nee* Jones) |
| 1399 | John le Graunt | 1732 | John Langford |
| 1516 | Peter Graunt | 1746 | Charles Langford |
| 1568 | Stephen Bord | 1780 | John Borrer |
| 1623 | Henry Chatfield | 1796 | James Lloyd |
| 1669 | Edward Jones, junr. | | |

### Northbarns

| | | | |
|---|---|---|---|
| ? | William Blackman | 1732 | John Langford |
| 1649 | Richard Streater | 1746 | Charles Langford |
| 1667 | John Streater | 1780 | John Borrer |
| 1667 | Edward Jones, snr. | 1783 | William Borrer |
| 1672 | Edward Jones, junr. | 1796 | James Lloyd |
| 1729 | Frances Young (*nee* Jones) | | |

### Malthouse

| | | | |
|---|---|---|---|
| ?1679 | Frances Jones | 1780 | John Borrer |
| 1729 | Frances Young (*nee* Jones) | 1783 | William Borrer |
| 1732 | John Langford | 1796 | James Lloyd |
| 1746 | Charles Langford | | |

### Flood's

| | | | |
|---|---|---|---|
| ? | Thomas Flood | 1658 | Edward Jones, snr. |
| 1641 | Judith Flood | 1672 | Edward Jones, junr. |
| 1658 | Thomas and Judith Heyward | | (from then on as Northbarns) |

By 1804 all the farms had lost their individual identities and the farmhouses of Flood's and Grant's Farms had probably been demolished. However, at the time of writing some evidence has been found which suggests that the Posting House (see Chapter Four, No. 61) is Grant's farmhouse. As yet it is still not absolutely certain and more detailed research is needed before a conclusion is reached. This would, of course, account for the lack of early information on the Posting House.

### Old and New Salts Farms

These two farms are dealt with in the next chapter as their origin is connected with the reclaiming of the marshlands.

### Lancing Rectory Estate

In 1350 Michael de Poynings, William Fifhide and others granted to the Prior and brothers of the religious house of

Mottenden in Headcorn, Kent, the great tithes of Lancing together with half an acre of land and the advowson of Lancing church. Mottenden had been founded in 1224 by an earlier Sir Michael de Poynings[120] and was dedicated to the Holy Trinity. It was the first house of the Trinitarians or Maturine Friars to be founded in England.

In 1362 in an inquisition it was stated that the King gave licence to Michael de Poynings and others to grant the half acre of land and advowson of the church as mentioned above and that the Monastery of Mottenden was to find two chaplains to pray for the welfare of the King during his life, for his soul after his death, and also for the souls of the ancestors and heirs of both the King and Michael. It was also stated that the half acre of land and advowson were parcel of the Manor of Lancing which was held by Nigel de Brok from the Lord of Bramber (John de Mowbray) by knight's service. The land was valued at 3d. per acre, and the church at £23 6s. 8d. per annum.[121]

A further link between the monastery and Lancing was the name of a minister at Mottenden in 1470, Richard de Lancing, who added to the Mottenden library two volumes which are now in the Bodleian Library. One book contains the note 'Bought by Friar Richard de Lancing, 1467, price 26/8 but it is worth more'.[122]

The monastery continued to appoint the vicars until Henry VIII ordered the Suppression of the Monasteries, and in 1538 Thomas Cromwell managed to acquire Lancing rectory, advowson of the church, the great tithes, the land granted to the monastery, and other glebe lands (mentioned in 1298).[123]

In 1547 the estate passed to the Bishop of Lincoln[124] and by 1573 consisted of a house, 20 acres of land and tithes.[125] In 1650 Henry Bartellot of Stopham apparently held the lease, and in 1662 his son Walter was the impropriator.[126] It appears that the lease then descended in the family, being held at three lives[127] until it was sold to the Reverend Edward Martin, whose daughter and heir Elizabeth (died 1790) married James Lloyd (died 1798). James Martin Lloyd (son of James) purchased the fee simple from the Bishop of Lincoln.[128] After the Enclosure Act in 1803 the 20 acres of land became absorbed into the Lloyd's estates and was no longer recognisable as a separate estate.

*Chapter Three*

## DEVELOPMENT OF LAND AND FIELD NAMES

MAPS SHOWING the field names in Lancing have been prepared from many references in old deeds and documents and by consulting all the known maps of Lancing. Several of the furlong names are still missing and others can only be located approximately in their areas.

The first map (Lancing, *c.* 1800) depicts the outline of the main fields and shows four areas. A larger scale map of each of these areas has been produced showing the minor fields, furlongs and other relevant information.

The layout of Lancing shown in the area maps is that which obtained a few years prior to the Division and Enclosure Act. Fields which were enclosed before 1800 are shown shaded. Those unshaded are the common fields. The fields not identified before the date of the map have been given the name which appears on the 1838 Tithe Map of Lancing. The names of the blocks of copyhold lands lying in the common fields are those allotted and shown on the enclosure map of Lancing dated 1803. Many of the old copyhold names date back prior to the 16th century. They have retained their names although ownership has changed. Prior to 1803 these old copyhold lands lying in the common fields were scattered throughout the parish. Under the Enclosure Act, blocks of land equivalent in acreage were allocated to the new owners.

It is most likely that a considerable area of Lancing was originally covered with trees. Initially the areas immediately above and below the village, centreing on Manor Road, were cleared of trees, but gradually the clearing process included land further away to the north and south of the village, as more land was required for agricultural purposes or for grazing.

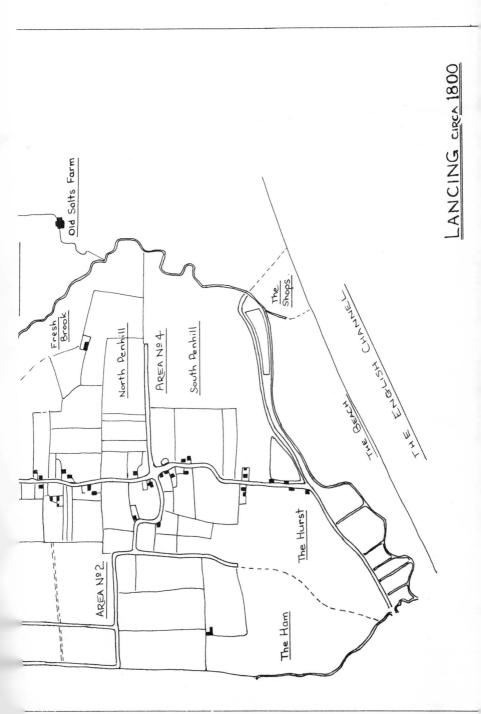

The large fields thus formed were later known as the Upper and
Lower West Laines and East Laine respectively. These formed
the basis of a three-field system of agriculture which was
common in this part of Sussex.

It appears from the old maps of Lancing that the road now
known as Crabtree Lane was a path which, at one time, was
the southern extremity of Lower West Laine. Later this lower
portion was extended further southwards and what is now the
modern Sompting Road (leading west from the railway station)
formed the southern boundary. This is borne out by the fact
that the remaining areas south of Sompting Road were once
known as the Hurst and the Ham.

Old deeds inform us that the Upper and Lower West Laines
and East laine were the common fields of Lancing and were
sub-divided into furlongs. The word furlong is derived from
'furrow-long' and originally represented the amount of land,
one furrow long, in a field of 10 acres, where the acre was
4,840 square yards. The length of the furrow was 220 yards,
or one-eighth of a mile.[1] The sides and ends of each furlong
were often used as paths for access to the intermixed strips.
Many of these paths eventually became roads or lanes, such
as First Avenue (originally Church Path), West Lane, Crabtree
Lane, Sompting Road, Grinstead Lane, North Road, and
South Street.

The system of agriculture involving individual strips of land
was utilised in Lancing until 1805, when the Division and
Enclosure Act of George III had been implemented. Each
landowner was allotted whole fields or area of land equal to
the amount of strips he held. These fields could be enclosed
by means of hedges, fences, or ditches. This in itself eventually led to the disappearance of many of the furlong names
as many farms became self-contained 'estates' and the old
names were no longer necessary for identification purposes.
Prior to the official Enclosure Act, many enclosures had been
carried out in Lancing, often causing hardship and loss of
common grazing rights to the poorer inhabitants of Lancing,
while increasing the wealth and power of the lord of the manor.

The 'inning' or reclaiming of the marshlands in Lancing is
an example of large-scale enclosing, which is described in detail

later. In Tudor times a great deal of enclosing was carried out. Names such as 'parks', 'intakes', 'breaks', 'breaches' or 'new fields' all indicated land which was previously wooded, waste, derelict or marshland. Lancing contains several such examples which aid in identifying the enclosures to Tudor times. Often the people who helped or were responsible for clearing the land obtained part or all of it. This land is thus identifiable because it invariably took the owner's name.

### Notes on Field Names and Other Features shown on the Maps
### The following names appear on Map of Area, No. 1
*Mill Furlong*

This name was given to the furlong which was adjacent to the mill. Mill Road now commemorates the fact that it was once the lane or path leading to the mill.

*Hampshire Furlong*

It is possible that this name was derived from the position of the furlong which was on the west or 'Hampshire' side of the mill furlong. It is more likely, however, that it was derived from the 'Hempshares' furlong, a field in which hemp was grown and allotted or shared out.

*Chalk Pit*

An extract from the enclosure award of Lancing in 1805 adequately describes the use of the chalk pit: '. . . a public chalk pit for the use of all proprietors and occupiers of lands and heriditaments in the Parish of Lancing to be by them expended or used for building and repairing of buildings and the manuring of lands in the said parish . . .'. However, early in the 20th century a person was killed while removing chalk, and the practice has now been forbidden by law.

*The Links Furlong*

The word 'links' is derived from Old English and means 'ridge'. The area represented by the Links Furlong is mainly that portion of land now covered by the Manor Recreation

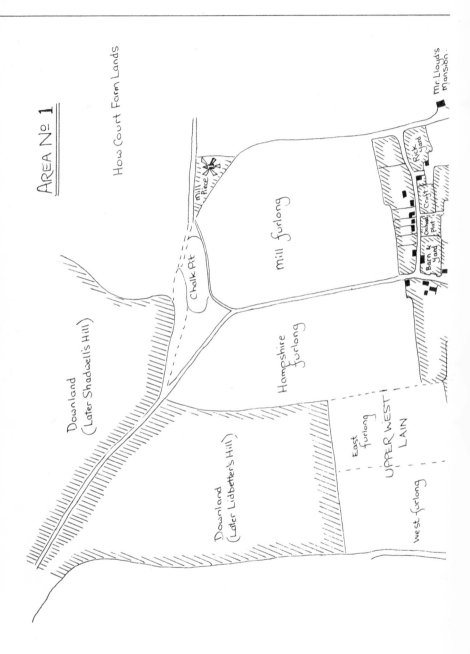

AREA № 1

How Court Farm Lands

Downland
(Later Shadwell's Hill)

Chalk Pit

Mill Piece

Mill furlong

Hampshire furlong

Downland
(Later Lidbetter's Hill)

East furlong

UPPER WEST LAIN

West furlong

Mr. Lloyd's Mansion

Rick Yard

Croft

Orchard Plot

Barn & Yard

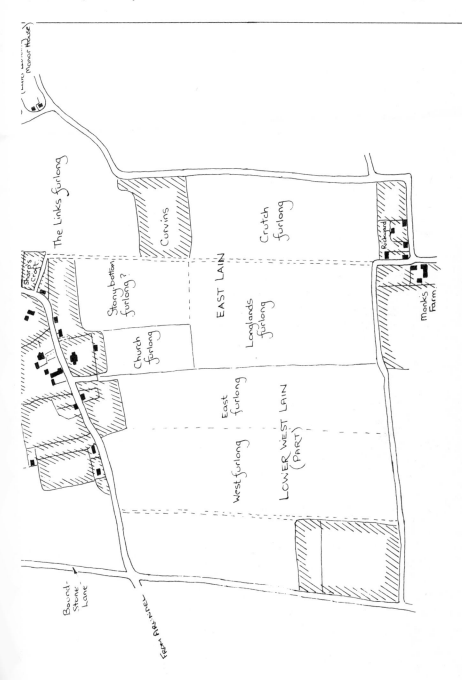

Ground. There is a ridge running west to east across the middle of the manor grounds where the land slopes down to a lower level. It is therefore possible that this ridge led to the name 'Links Furlong'. One theory is that the top of this ridge is thought to be the site of the suspected Roman road which originated in Chichester. The road supposedly passed across the manor to the south of the site of the old manor-house, to the rear of the Malthouse Cottage and Malthouse Farm and emerged at the junction of Hoe Court Lane and the old Upper Brighton Road. From there it passed along this road to the ferry across the River Adur, passing in turn through Shoreham and South-wick. However, it is more likely that the Roman road passed along the Street, which is to the north of the recreation ground.

*Crutch Furlong*

This is thought to be derived from the old word *cruch,* meaning a cross. However, no satisfactory explanation can be found for the meaning of a cross associated with this piece of land. There is a vague connection in that the furlong was adjacent to the path which led to the church.

**The following names appear on Map of Area, No. 2**
*Caper's Field*

No reference has been found to a person named Caper in Lancing. However, old deeds refer to a Caper's Field, which is shown, and a Caper's Gate. Gate in this instance probably meant entrance to a lane or path. An old inhabitant of Lancing told me that his grandfather knew the modern Crabtree Lane as Caper's Lane, no doubt the lane that led to Caper's Field.

*Bowell's Copyhold and Snelling's Croft Copyhold*

Bowell and Snelling are referred to as inhabitants of Lancing and How Court respectively during the 16th and 17th centuries. It is interesting to note that for many years, during the 20th century, a butcher's shop with the name 'Snelling' was situated in North Road to the west of the road, and was actually on the site of the old Snelling's croft, perhaps a descendant of the same family!

## The Ham

The word 'ham' means 'enclosure' or possibly in this case a meadow near water. In old Lancing many 'cow leases' (the right to graze cows) were available on 'the Hamm'. A barn was later erected, and part of the old lane which later led from the north entrance of Lancing Carriage Works was formerly Ham Lane and the access to the old barn.

## The Hurst

'Hurst' means 'a wooded area' and no doubt the Hurst was originally covered with trees. Eventually it was cleared and used for agricultural purposes. In 1805 the Ham and the Hurst were awarded to J. M. Lloyd, and his family retained this land. Nearly one hundred years later in 1903, 130 acres of this land were sold to the London, Brighton and South Coast Railway (L.B. & S.C.R.) for £21,683 2s. 6d. This was later to become the Lancing Carriage Works (now the Churchill Industrial Estate).

## The following names appear on Map of Area, No. 3

### Church Farm Brooks

Church Farm Brooks was marshland originally known, in 1591, as How Plattes (Flats). Later this land became part of Church Farm and was renamed Church Farm Brooks.

### Malthouse Brook

This was marshland to the east of the Broad Dam and Church Farm Brooks, known as the How End Brook in 1591.

Both of the above pieces of marshland indicate a strong connection with the original manor of How. This is so because the Howlaine was the common field for the manor of How and if earlier buildings existed on or near the site of the Malthouse Farm then they would probably be in the manor of How and not Lancing. Consequently the marshes opposite (i.e., How Plattes and the How End Marsh) could then have been considered as common pastureland of the inhabitants of How, as indeed it was in the latter part of the 16th century.

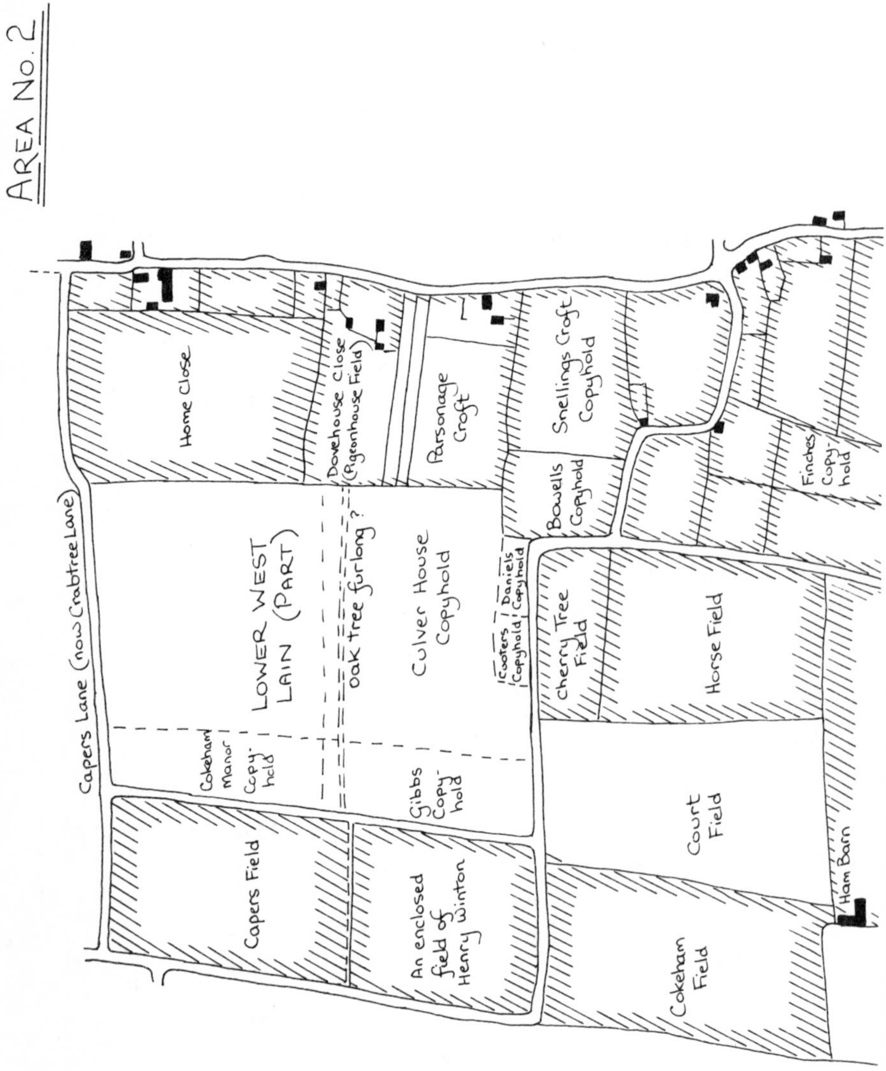

AREA No. 2

Capers Lane (now Crabtree Lane)

Home Close

Dovehouse Close (Pigeonhouse Field)

Parsonage Croft

Snellings Croft Copyhold

Finches Copyhold

Bowells Copyhold

LOWER WEST LAIN (PART)

Oak tree furlong?

Culver House Copyhold

Cooters / Daniels Copyhold / Copyhold

Cherry Tree Field

Horse Field

Cokeham Manor Copyhold

Gibbs Copyhold

Capers Field

An enclosed field of Henry Winton

Court Field

Cokeham Field

Ham Barn

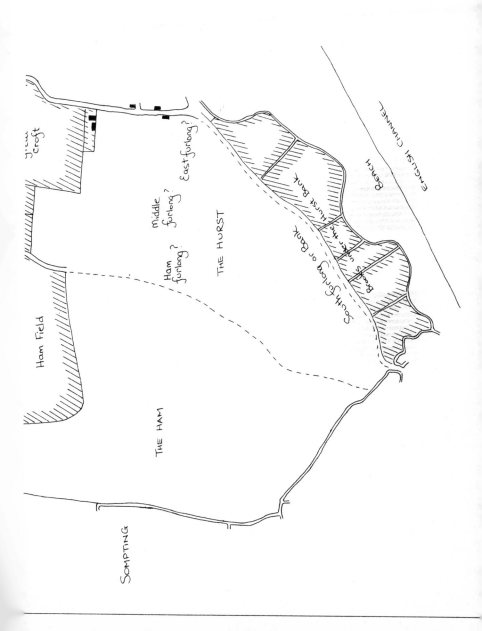

*Carter's Park, Daniel's Field, and Gibb's Field*

These areas have taken the names of former inhabitants of Lancing, who were no doubt either instrumental in clearing the lands and aiding in the 'inning' of the area from the sea in the 16th century, or held the land at some later date.

A Harry Carter is mentioned in the Lancing Churchwardens Presentments in 1624,[2] and John Carter in lists of inhabitants in 1641.[3] John William Daniel[4] is shown as a witness to a survey in 1608.

*Bury Brook, Borough's Three-Acres, Borough's Two-Three
   Roods*

Once part of the land of the Burry or Burré family of Lancing and Sompting, Bury and Borough are later corruptions of the family name. Bury's Brook was known as Ryman's in 1662, and was formerly part of the estate of the Streater family of Lancing.

*Bury's and Shadwell's Nimbles*

These two pieces of marshland are probably part of a large area once known as North and South Nimbles in the 16th century. Later owners retained part of the old name and preceded 'Nimbles' with their own names to identify them. Bury is a corruption of Burré or Burry family. Shadwell is mentioned below. The word 'Nimble' seems to have originated from the Greek word meaning pasture.

*Shadwell's Curvins, Shadwell's Eight-Acre Brook*

Part of the farmlands of a Mr. Shadwell in the latter part of the 18th century. (Sold to J. M. Lloyd in 1796.)

*Inner and Outer Bulmans*

Part of an old farm in Lancing known as Bulmans. A deed of 1658 refers to an 'old house called Bulmans old house with a gateroome on the North adjoining the street'.

*Washer's Copyhold*

This piece of marshland, which originally must have belonged to a person named Washer, lies right in the middle of the North Nimbles, which in 1591 was occupied by a person named Washer. This is mentioned in detail later in the chapter.

*Cooter's Copyhold*

A family with the name of Cooter lived in Lancing in the 18th century and a member was probably connected with this piece of land.

*Barn Field*

The field in which 'old Marsh Barn' is situated. The barn is situated in the area known in 1591 as the 'Old Marshes'. The original lane leading to the barn was known as the 'Marsh Lane'. The modern name 'Mash Barn Lane' is obviously a corruption of this.

*How Laine*

This field was originally the common field for the inhabitants of the Manor of How (Hoecourt). The modern Hoe Court Lane leads up the west side of the middle furlong. No mention of a west furlong has been found, but it is most probable that it was part or all of the land to the west of Hoe Court Lane.

*Mill Field*

An enclosed field so named because it was opposite an early Lancing windmill. (See chapter on 'Old Buildings of Lancing').

*Crooked Acre*

This name was probably derived from its shape rather than its area, as it is, in fact, approximately five acres in extent.

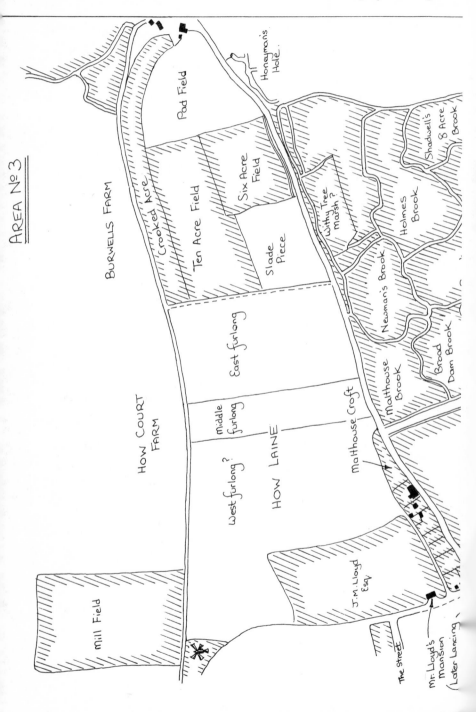

Area Nº 3

Mill Field

How Court Farm

Burwells Farm

West furlong ?

middle furlong

East furlong

How Laine

Crooked Acre

Ten Acre Field

Slade Piece

Six Acre Field

Pad Field

Honeyman's Hole.

Withy Tree marsh ?

Newman's Brook

Holmes Brook

Shadwell's 8 Acre Brook

Malthouse Brook

Broad Dam Brook

Malthouse Croft

J. M. Lloyd Esqʳ.

The Street

Mr. Lloyd's Mansion (Later Lancing ...

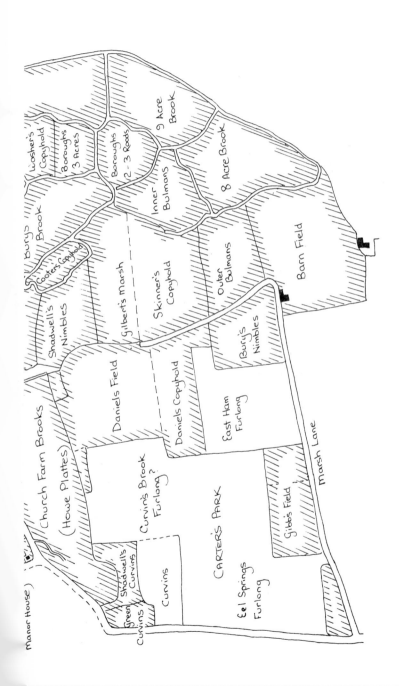

*Slade Piece*

One of the meanings for the word 'slade' is 'an open country', and possibly Slade Piece simply means a piece of open ground.

*Honeyman's Hole*

There have been many tales in Lancing concerning this water-filled hole. Stories of old stagecoaches disappearing with everybody on board drowned were quite common in my childhood. Other names were given to the hole, such as the 'Bottomless Pit' and 'Adam's Hole'.

Originally it was a large pool of water formed when a wall was built from the road down to Old Salts Farm, enclosing or 'inning' the marshes, and was probably the pool known as the Ryde in a court case of 1591.[6] It was later or likewise known as the 'Weald Ditch', 'Well Dyke' or 'Wall Dyke'. Over the years it became smaller, and ended up as an inconspicuous pond when the A27 was formed.

In 1644 a Thomas Honiman resided in Lancing and was probably in some way connected with this pool.

*Withy Tree Marsh*

A withy tree is a variety of willow and at present there are some willows still to be seen at the side of the road to the north of this piece of marshland. After the 1939–45 war pre-fabricated houses were erected on this site, and the place was known as 'Withy Patch'.

**The following names appear on Map of Area, No. 4**

*Speercroft*

This name appears to have been derived from the shape of the field which is somewhat similar in shape to a spearhead. At the eastern end of the field were six cottages (shown on the map) known as Botany Bay houses, no doubt due to their remote position. By 1838 these cottages were gone, and no details as to their construction and the date of their erection are available. It is quite possible they were built by squatters.

*Pound Plat*

Probably the site of the village pound.

*Lime Pits Furlong*

The site originally occupied by lime pits which were used for agricultural purposes.

*Capenham Furlong*

This name presents some difficulty regarding its origin. 'Ham' in this case probably means an enclosure, linked with a capon (chicken), or the name could have been derived from the old family of Capon who resided in Lancing in the 15th and 16th centuries. This would mean that Capon's Ham later became corrupted to Capenham.

*Blackman's, Blackman's Breach, Pengarden, etc.*

As mentioned previously, there were many Tudor enclosures of which the above three were examples. The New Field is another example, and all around this area are pieces of copyhold land which were probably awarded to the other people who helped in the clearing of the land. Skinner, Lees, Blackman and Pallingham are all names which belong to residents of Lancing during the 16th and 17th centuries.

*Watchhouse Furlong*

In this vicinity was the original tower-like structure (shown on the map) which was prepared for the defence of the Sussex coast against the Spanish Armada. These structures supported brushwood, which would be lit when the Armada was sighted. They were placed on prominent points all over Sussex, e.g., at Chanctonbury and Ditchling Beacon. They were sometimes referred to as 'watchhouses', and it is logical to assume that Watchhouse Furlong would be sited nearby.

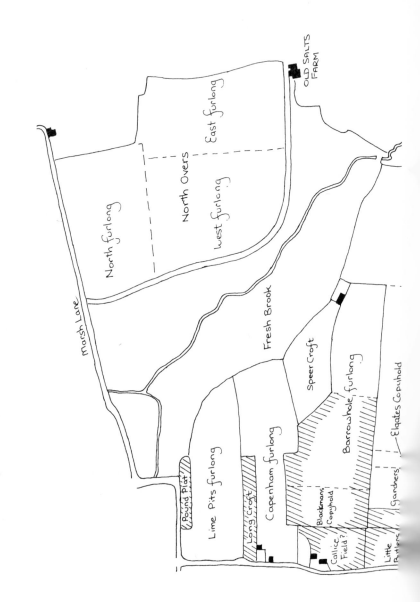

Area No. 4

Marsh Lane

North furlong

North Overs

West furlong

East furlong

OLD SALTS FARM

Fresh Brook

Speer Croft

Barrowhole furlong

Elgates Copyhold

Gardners

Pound Plat

Lime Pits furlong

Long Croft

Capenham furlong

Blackmans Copyhold

Callice Field?

Little Butlers

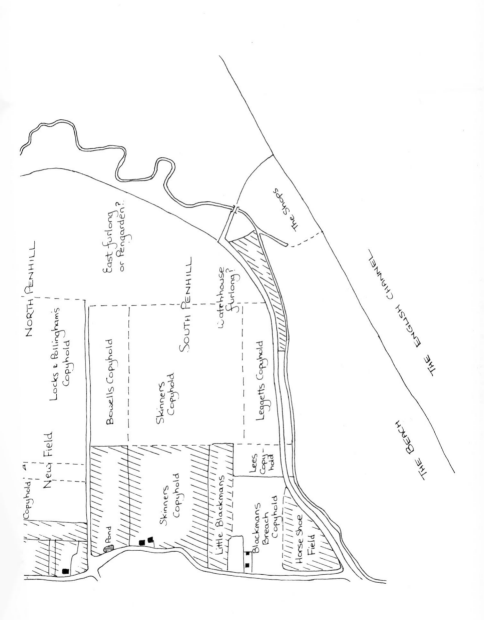

North Penhill

South Penhill

East furlong?
or Pengarden?

Waterhouse
furlong?

The Shoars

THE ENGLISH CHANNEL

THE BEACH

Locks & Billinghams
Copyhold

Bowells Copyhold

Skinners
Copyhold

Leggetts Copyhold

New Field

Copyhold?

Skinners
Copyhold

Little Blackmans

Lees
Copy-
hold

Blackmans
Breach
Copyhold

Horse Shoe
Field

Pond

## The Development of the Marshlands

*Old and New Salt's Farms*

The diagrams shown facilitate descriptions of the marsh area. Settlements named in Diagram No. 1 are marked only as crosses in the remainder of the diagrams, as datum points. Diagram No. 1 shows the possible coastline, *c.* 1085, and is derived from

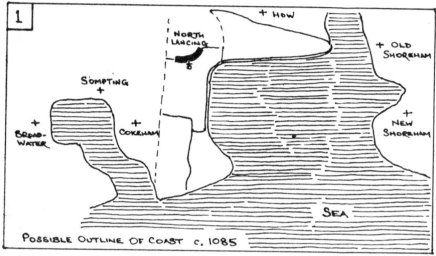

Diagram 1:   Possible outline of the coast, *c.*1085.

the later facts about and development of Lancing. A large estuary of the Adur flowed across the area now occupied by Shoreham airfield, Old and New Salt's farms, and Monk's farm.

Another expanse of water flowed past Cokeham up to Sompting and Broadwater. These areas contained salt marshes at low tide, where the salt pans of the Domesday Book were probably situated, and were directly open to the sea.

Diagram No. 2 shows the probable outline, *c.* 1250, when there are mentions of the port of Pende. The beach is shown as having cut off the direct access to the Great Broadwater and forming a protective barrier by Pende Hill (Penhill) in Lancing, behind which was estimated the site of the ancient port of Pende. It is most probable that more land existed in

Lancing to the south and east of Pende Hill originally, as Nonae Returns for 1340 relating to Lancing show a depreciation in value between 1340 and the earlier returns of 1292 due to the loss of land, a watermill, and 70 salthouses to the sea during the intervening 48 years.[5]

The eastward drift of the shingle no doubt caused the gradual silting up of the west side of the old estuary (near Grinstead

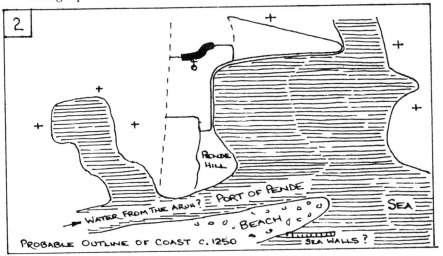

Diagram 2: Probable outline of the coast, *c.*1250.

Lane) and the old Pende harbour, which was probably responsible for its closure as a port at the end of the 15th century. Diagrams Nos. 3-6 were compiled from the information contained in an old court case of 1591,[6] in the time of Queen Elizabeth I. From the recordings of the case, together with information from two later maps[7] it was evident that, *c.* 1500, streams ran across the marshes at low tide, one in particular flowing on the south side of the old Upper Brighton Road (then the north bank of the salt marshes), ending at the top of Grinstead Lane. Another stream flowing north-westwards from the great channel (see Diagram No. 3) joined this stream and formed a pool almost opposite the bottom of Hoe Court Lane; both the stream and the pool were known as the Ryde. This was an old word meaning a channel intermittently filled with water.

During the 16th century a great deal of reclaiming or 'inning' was carried out by the lord of the manor of Lancing to the detriment of the inhabitants who lost convenient common land. The inning consisted of erecting a high bank or wall to keep out the water at high tide, but with a sluice to allow draining of the marshland, usually from a dyke, at low tide. The tops of these walls were often used as paths, and some eventually became roads. The land inned in this way was later rented to tenants by the lord of the manor.

Due to this inning the inhabitants of How (Hoecourt) eventually lost some of their rights of common and so in 1591 Thomas Sherley, lord of the manor of Hoecourt, brought an action against Sir Henry Goring, lord of the manor of 'North Launsinge and Mounckes, alias South Launsinge' and John Blackman, William Woode and Nicholas Washer, who were apparently tenant farmers. The case was heard on 30 and 31 March 'in the XXXIII yere of the rayne of oure Soverayne Lady Elizabeth . . . before Thomas Bishoppe, Richard Bellingham, Giles Garton and Thomas Churcher, gent.'.

One of the earliest parts of the marshlands to be inned was the 'Fresh Brook (see Diagram No. 3), which was a stream flowing from the Great Channel to the north-west terminating

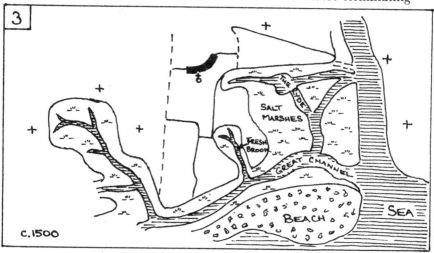

Diagram 3:   Outline of the coast, *c.* 1500.

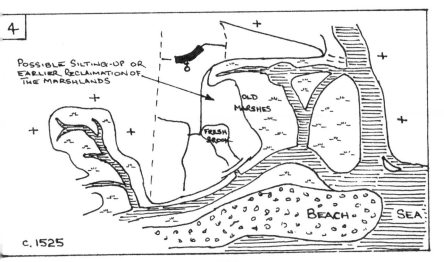

Diagram 4: Outline of the coast, *c*. 1525.

near the junction of the present Mash Barn Lane and Grinstead Lane. The Fresh Brook was inned by building a wall joining the rising grounds of Old Salt's Farm to the cliff on which houses overlooking the junction of Old Salts Farm Road and Brighton Road now stand. This wall eventually became Old Salts Farm Road (see Diagram No. 4.).

From the Interogateries and Depositions contained in the court case a good picture of the development of the inning of the salt marshes emerges. John Stempe of Launsinge, Yeoman, aged 79, a witness in the case 'sayth he knoweth a parcell of land in Lawnsynge called ye Freshe brooke ever synce he could remember and that he never knew it unwalled, and yt as well as ye Queenes Tennauntes as all other ye Tennaunts and occupyers of landes in both Lawnsynges hathe common there for there chattell from Lammas Daye to St. Davyes Daye and yt the Farmer hathe ye proffit there of ye rest of ye year and this they do at this presente enjoye savinge yt Sir Henrye Goringes Farmer as he thinketh hathe of late encroched uppon ye sayde lande by plowinge abowte twoe acres as he esteemeth it'.

Assuming that John Stempe could remember back to when he was about six years old then this would put the inning at about the year 1518. However, other witnesses in the case put a latest date at about 1531, and so *c*. 1525 would seem an appropriate date to settle for. It must be mentioned here that the original documents of the court case are mutilated and damaged in places or are illegible and so only some of the pages were copied. This does make certain areas, which are mentioned in the case, difficult to locate exactly.

The next areas to be inned were lying around the Ryde, and William Swyfte, another witness in the case, 'a fisherman of the age of three score and sixe yeres' said that 'he knoweth the water called the Ryde and that before the Innynge of the mershes the salt water did flowe upp to the mershe banke in the occupacyon of William Androse widdowe'. (Mrs. Andrews lived where the Malthouse Farm stood.) He continued by saying 'that the lande of Mr. Sherley sometyme in the occupacyon of one Robertes and Robert Whittingeton sometyme occupyer of ye lande nowe in the occupacyon of one John Capon have used to common uppon the lande nowe known by the name of Hydes brooke, Blackman's brooke, Capons brooke and Peeters brooke before suche tyme as the same brooks weare Inned from the seas, and he saythe that Sir William Goringe did Inne the sayde lande, but, howe longe synce this deponent cannott certaynelye remember'.

Before the inning this marshland was known as How Plattes and at low tide was used as common for sheep and cattle of the inhabitants of Hoe Court only. The inhabitants of Lancing had to keep to the south of the Ryde, as William Swyfte tells us when he goes on to say 'that the water called the Ryde did devyde the sayde brookes from the residue of ye mershes and when the sheepe or cattell of the Tenants of Lawnsinge did come over ye sayde Ryde they were allwayes driven backe agayne and manye tymes the boyes weare beaten for there negligence in Sufferinge [it], and this he dothe knowe for yt himselfe was borne in ye said parishe of Lawnsynge, and when he was a boye kept sheepe over agaynste ye same in the mershes'.

Sir William Goring inned this piece of marshland *c.*1543 and then put in tenants for rents; in this case the tenants in 1591 were Capon and Peeter, who were inhabitants of Hoe

Court, Blackman from Lancing, and Hyde, a tenant of the
Queen's Manor of St. John's in Lancing. The inning of this
piece was achieved by building a wall from the main road,
slightly to the west and opposite Hoe Court Lane, down

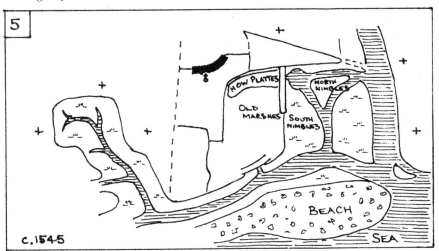

Diagram 5:   Outline of the coast, *c.*1545.

towards Mash Barn Lane (see Diagram No. 5). This wall, known
in 1555 as 'Whyttington's Damme',[8] was later called the Broad
Dam. This inning is also confirmed by John Stempe who
mentions the Ryde, which 'did in tyme paste flowe upp unto
the Baye or Damme which devydeth a mershe nowe in the
occupation of William Androse widdowe nowe called Howe
end and that when the sayde Damme did breake it did flowe
up to a place called Kelvins [Kervins or Curvins] and himself
hath rowed upp thyther in a corke'. He confirms that only
Hoe Court tenants used How Plattes, when he stated that
'Howe Courte and fower other howses in Howe within the
parishe of West Grinstead aforesayde onelye did use to common
together in Hydes brooke, Blakeman's brooke, Capon Brooke,
and Peeter's Brooke, as they are nowe called for that they nowe
doe occupye them which before the sayde Innings were called
Howe Plattes, and that tyme owte of mynde before the same
were Inned the Tennauntes of Howe Courte did common and

keep their sheepe and other cattell there when it was lowe
water, butt howe long agon the same were Inned he cannot
certaynely saye butt thinketh it to be above fiftye yeres agoe ...
and all this knew the better for that he was borne and did
dwell neare adjoyninge to ye same and his Father occupyed
much of the sayde lande'. Later this piece of marshland is
shown as Church Farm brooks.

At about the same time as the above inning (the date is not
very clear from the court case) the 'old marshes' were inned. It
appears that this was the marshland to the south of the Ryde
as mentioned above (see also Diagram No. 5). How this piece
of salt marsh was enclosed is not quite clear, but it appears
quite probable that it was a continuation southwards of the
previously mentioned Broad Dam until it meets slightly higher
ground leading from the Old Salts Farm area. Later names of
parts of this marshland, i.e., Carter's Park and Daniel's Field,
were certainly connected with inhabitants of Lancing.

The court case did not refer to any other inning by Sir
William Goring, who died in 1553, and his son, Sir Henry
Goring, inherited the manor and carried on in his father's
footsteps according to the depositions in the court case. The
next piece of marshland identified was known as the North
and South Nimbles. In later documents the Nimbles are described as part of the Old Marshlands and so one can assume
that the Old Marshlands must have been a general name for
all the old marshes previously reclaimed during the 16th century. Some further information is given when another witness
in the case, William Hyde of Lawnsinge, yeoman, aged 50, said
'he knoweth the mershe in Lawnsinge called ye Sowthe and
Northe Nymbles, and that the Queenes Tennauntes of St
Joanes [John's] and Sir Henry Goryng's Tennauntes did allwayes use to common there together until ye Innynge thereof
which was above sixteen years paste, and ye Sayde Tennauntes
have kept their chattell and sheepe there as in the right of
there Tenements, and nowe neyther ye Queenes Tennauntes
nor Sir Henry Goringes tennauntes have anye Common in ye
said southe and northe nymbles for yt ye sayd Sir Henry
Goringe hathe demised ye same in Farme by lease'. William
Hyde was a tenant of the Queen's Manor of St. John's and as

he said it was over sixteen years since the inning we can assume
it took place in about 1575. We are able to pinpoint the two
areas as William Swyfte mentions the tenants in 1591 when
he says, 'he knoweth ye landes called ye Southe and Northe
Nymbles in ye parish of Lawnsinge and is nowe in ye occupacyon of olde Stempe and one Washer . . .'. The map of
Area No. 3 shows us Washer's copyhold to the north of the
Ryde and Shadwell's and Bury's Nimbles to the south. This
piece of inning was carried out by building a wall from the
main highway (near the *Sussex Pad*) which went southwards
and then south-west to join up with the higher ground near
the present Old Salts Farmhouse (see Diagram No. 6). In
several instances during the court case it was mentioned that
Sir William Goring had already built a long high bank along the
north of the marshlands parallel to the highway previous to
1553, and it was to this that the wall enclosing the North and
South Nimbles was joined at its east end. Since the Ryde could
no longer flow up to the Broad Dam, near Hoe Court Lane,
and a sluice gate in the wall drained the marshes at low tide,
a pool formed to the east of the newly-formed wall in 1575.
This pool was later shown as the weald dyke, wall dyke or
well dyke, and later still as Honiman's hole.

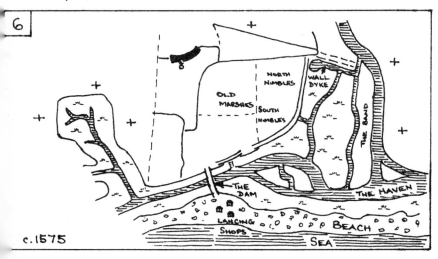

Diagram 6: Outline of the coast, *c.*1575.

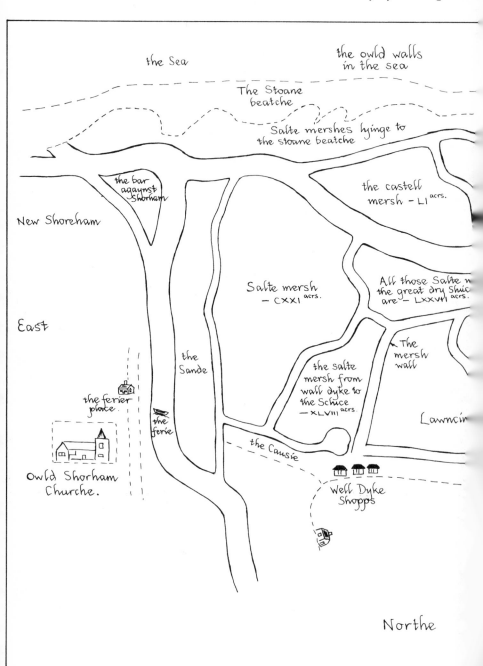

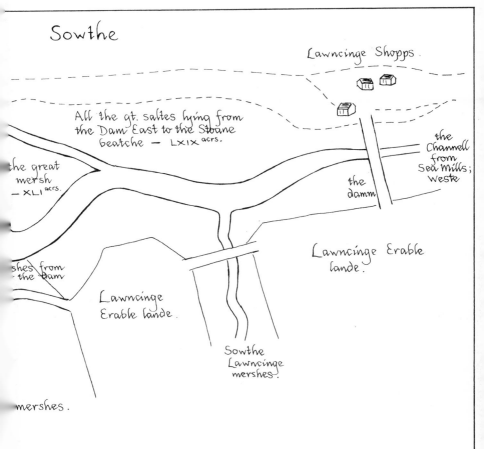

Sowthe

Lawncinge Shopps.

All the gt. saltes lying from
the Dam East to the Stoane
beatche — LXIX acrs.

the
Channell
from
Sea Mills;
Weste

the great
mersh
— XLI acrs.

the
damm

shes from
the Dam

Lawncinge Erable
lande.

Lawncinge
Erable lande.

Sowthe
Lawncinge
mershes.

mershes.

all the salte mershes lyinge on the Sowthe
Syde of the great Channell to the Stoane beatche are:— 161 acres.
all the mershes lyinge on the northe Syde of
the gret Sewer to well Dyke between the Sande
and Lawncinge wall are :- — 246 acres.
Sum of acrage of all
thes Salte mershes — 407 acres.

LANCING MARSHES circa 1600
(Based partly on a map held in the Marlipins
Museum, Shoreham, surveyor and date
unknown and partly on a map by George
Randoll, 1622 held at Petworth House Archives)

Two other smaller innings were carried out to the south of the marshlands near the sea and both were referred to in the court case. The first piece was known as the 'new marshes', which were pieces of marshland either side of the Great Channel to the west of the present Shopsdam Road. A further witness in the case, Robert Capon of Launsinge, 'sayth that he knoweth the mersh ground in Launsinge called the new mershe and yt was used a common to keepe sheepe and other cattell but for what Tennauntes he knoweth not and since the ynninge thereof which is about XXtie yeres past yt hath not byn used as a common and this he knoweth bycause he hath eversince byn dwellinge in Launsinge and XXtie years before'. This piece was inned by building a dam across the channel near the junction of the present Old Salts Farm Road. The dam is, in fact, now known as Shopsdam Road as it eventually became the path or road to the fishermen's shops on the beach. This inning can be put at about 1571.

The most recent inning referred to was that at South Lancing when William Swyfte said 'he knoweth the grene at the streat end under the Cliffe of South Launsinge and there hathe gon tyme owte of memorye of man a hye waye for carte and carryadge through the same green and the sayde Cliffe, greene and way hathe always ben common for the Queenes Tennauntes and other of the parishioners of Launsynge to feede there cattell and sheepe there', and he goes on to say: 'and there was a common watering place which the Tenants did allwayes use for wateringe of there cattell and now a very small parte thereof is left for the Tennauntes to water there cattell there, and the said Sir Henry Goringes Tenants of Monckes had within this yere or two enclosed and ploughed the sayde hye waye and greene for ye which he has payned at the Hundred Courte and forced to laye it open againe, and yett nevertheless the sayde Sir Henry Gorings Tennauntes have plowed it upp and sowed with wheate parte of the sayde greene this yere'. At the end of South Street in South Lancing was a small cliff which was known as the Bank in 1803 (Bank Cottage was built there), and there were fields to the south of this. Here, we are told, in about 1589 or 1590, is the start of some more inning. The later enclosure and tithe maps of Lancing show enclosed marshland at South Lancing around this area and so presumably Sir Henry Goring, or his son, must have continued the inning. There is no further reference to inning in this court case, and so we finish with what is a most interesting document, giving us information about the reclamation of the marshland which would probably have not been recorded if the court case had not taken place.

It is interesting to note, however, that during the court case there were references to 'saltcoates. (in the old marshes) which were storage places for salt. The position of some of these salt pans were discovered in a recent archaeological dig (see Chapter One). They were found in what has been shown as the North Nimbles (see Diagram No. 5).

The map of Lancing Marshes, *c.* 1600, has been drawn from two interesting maps,[7] one dated 1622, and held in Petworth House Archives, and the other, an undated map in the Marlipins Museum at Shoreham, estimated as having been drawn *c.* 1590. The original maps are, as yet, the earliest maps showing areas of Lancing. The original spelling and similar style of writing has been preserved on the copy. It is most likely that the undated map was made in preparation for the future innings of the marshes. Diagram No. 7 was compiled mainly from this map.

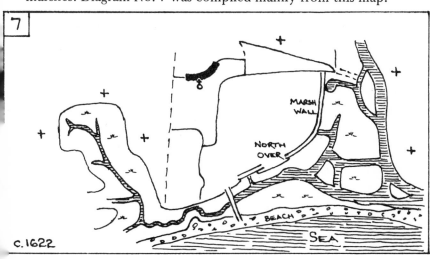

Diagram 7: Outline of the coast, *c.* 1622.

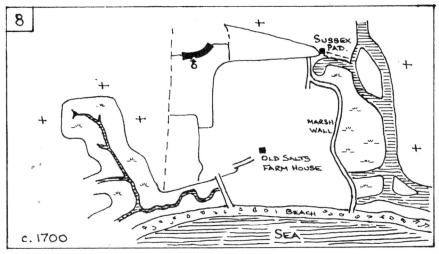

Diagram 8:   Outline of the coast, *c.* 1700.

There appears to be no more evidence of innings of the marshes until quite late in the 17th century, when in 1684 Sir William Goring embanked 600 acres of land at an expense of £600, by which a farm called The Salts (now known as Old Salts Farm) became part of his Manor of Lancing (see Diagram No. 8). Twelve years later in 1696 a commission was issued on the part of the Crown concerning this enclosure and to enquire into the derelict lands. However, the commissioners permitted the witnesses to 'drink so much wine, that they knew not what they swore, nor what verdict they gave'. The inquest was therefore discharged and taken off the file. No further claim has ever been instituted.[9]

It is interesting to note that in 1684 the cost of this land was £1 per acre and that in 1907 Old and New Salts Farms were sold for £30,000, or over £50 per acre.[10] One can only wonder what the price per acre would be today.

A large field to the north of Old Salts Farm is to this day called North Overs; in the 17th century deeds show this field to be the North Over. At first sight this appears to be a peculiar name for a field in the middle of marshes. However, *The Place Names of Sussex,* by Mawer and Stenton, informs us that the word 'over' is a derivative of the old German word *Ufer,* which means 'bank'. In this case the 'North Over' becomes the 'North Bank'. Diagram No. 7 shows that at full tide this field would to all intents and purposes be the north bank of the Great Channel.

In the latter part of the 18th century (*c.* 1770) more inning took place after the course of the River Adur had changed slightly towards the Shoreham side (see Diagram No. 9). Subsequently New Salts Farms developed. This no doubt caused Salts Farm to be renamed Old Salts Farm. By 1838 a few more fields had been added by producing another 'wall' which is now the present western bank of the River Adur.

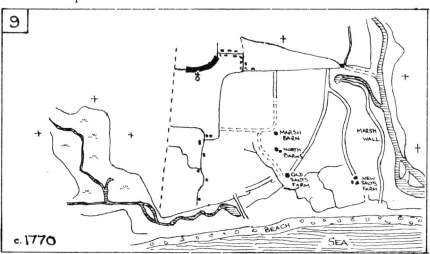

Diagram 9:   Outline of the coast, *c.* 1770.

The brooklands to the north of the road which leads from the *Sussex Pad* to the old toll bridge were part of the Salts Farm in 1758, when they were known as the 'New Inclosed Salts',[11] but when the Tithe Map was completed in 1838 these lands (about 63 acres) were shown as part of the Pad Farm; no doubt they were sold some time between these dates.

The author is indebted to Easter Estates, the present owners of Old and New Salts Farms, for the following notes regarding the history and development of the two farms.

Fig. 15. Old Barn—Old Salts Farm

The farms lay in the southern part of the River Adur valley.
Up to a few hundred years ago the river was not confined by
banks, and salt water spread over large areas of the low-lying
land in the valley. The land comprising the foreshore was not
protected from the sea, which at times washed away the mud
overlying the chalk and at others washed up large quantities
of sand, mud and gravel. This action continued for many years
over the low-lying ground back to the chalk hills. In some
places large quantities of beach were deposited and were subsequently covered with mud and sand.

In time the action of the sea during heavy storms rolled
seaweed, shingle and mud into a bank that still exists, south
of the Widewater; this bank has been artificially improved to
give additional protection against flooding. This was found
necessary owing to sea water passing under the original bank,
through the bed of beach and flooding the ground behind
the bank. This flooding is still apparent to a minor degree by
the rise and fall of the water in the Widewater.

. Old cottages, west of the *Farmer's Hotel*, pulled down in 1926. Standing at the gate
on the left are Mrs. Matten and Arthur Matten and at the right-hand gate, Mrs. Elsie Green.

Thatched cottages built by Charles Mason in 1926 on the same site as those shown in
top picture. They were demolished in 1974.

3. A view showing the corner in South Street formerly known as 'Trevett's Corner' due to Trevett's Sweet Shop which stood there for many years.

4. An early working scene at the old smithy, North Lancing with John Broomfield on the right and his son Alfred.

5. William Chorley, born 1848, died 22 November 1932 (founder of the Homes of Rest in Lancing).

6. (*above*) 'Channel View' Convalescent Home, formerly 'Stork's Nest', in South Lancing.

7. Lancing Windmill in 1904, showing signs of damage the year before it was pulled down.

8. Lancing Quoits Club in 1907. Quoits were played in the Brickfields off Penhill Road. *Back row l. to r.*: Eli Warr; Harry Falkenbridge; ? ; Charlie Matten; Billy Baggs; George Haller; Edwin Fuller; Mark Fuller. *Front row*: Tom Till; Cephas Gammans; George Humphrey; Charlie Humphrey; Sam Warr.

9. A view looking south down South Street from near the level-crossing. The Luxor Cinema now stands on the left by the hedge and most of the buildings are now gone.

10.  Farm workers in Lancing, 1910. *Left to right*: Luke Boyce; ? Hollingdale; Fred Sievier; Fred Gilbert; Fred Mitchell; Ted Merriott; Eli Warr.

11.  Mill Road with the Posting House visible behind the wall on the left. On the right is the Old Forge (with the door opened into the road) and Granary Cottage with thatched roof (demolished many years ago). The horse and cart belonged to Potter Bailey's of South Lancing.

12.  Old Tithe Barn, *c.* 1926, shortly after it was converted into a private residence. It was pulled down in 1963.

13.  A view from the Old Tithe Barn. The small building on the left is now a house (Barn Elms) but was orignally the stable for the Posting House in Mill Road. Colonel Goider's house is visible up Mill Road and on the right is part of Joyces Cottages in The Street.

14.  North Road. The Police Station now stands to the left and Addison Square to the right. Part of the old buildings in Monk's Farm can be seen further down the road on the left (now demolished).

15.  A copy taken from an old daguerrotype of Smith Cottage and the Old Forge, *c.* 1860. John Broomfield in the centre and Thomas Boniface Butler (furrier) on the right. The two younger boys were Butler's sons.

*Farrier*

16.  The Street, North Lancing, 1912. Joyces Cottages and Hawthorn Cottage can be seen on the left and on the right is the wall belonging to the Old Tithe Barn Property.

17. North Road. The Almshouses can be seen on the right as the building with two chimneys visible. The girls on the left are Eadie Green; May Merriott; Bessie Oram; Olive Cooper.

18. North Road shops just north of the station. The second shop is Bartlett's (Post Office). Woolworth's now stands in place of the wall and trees.

19.   Lancing Parish Council of 1910 on the lawns of Lancing Manor.

*Standing, from L to r.*: **C. F. Pyecroft**, nurseryman, Sompting Road. Developed Cecil Road, Lancing; **Thomas Lucking**, butcher, lived at 'Cherry Tree Cottage'; **Mr. Hardy**, retired gardener. Lived in Penhill Road; **W. G. Heaton**, headmaster of North Lancing School. Organist of Lancing Choir; **G. Fairs**, nurseryman in Freshbrook Road and Culver Road; **George Lisher**, coal merchant, Sompting Road. Hire cartage.

*Seated, from L to r.*: **W. S. Phillips**, farmer, Monks Farm, followed in 1913 by his son; **George Prideaux**, landlord of the *Three Horseshoes*. Followed by son and grandson; **James Cass**, farmer, Culver House, formerly grocer and landlord of the *Railway Hotel*; **James Martin Carr-Lloyd**, Lord of the Manor. Chairman of the Council, 1901–1919; **H. W. Doll**, of German origin. Lived at 'Forst Haus', North Road (now Woolworth's); **H. W. Danks**, commuter to London. Annual party given with magic lantern for children; **James Robinson**, clerk, market garden.

20. First motorised trade vehicle used in Lancing. 'Laddie' Trevett at the wheel with his son standing by the bonnet.

21. South Street. Colebourne's shop on the corner of Penhill Road.

22. A view of Lancing Manor House (pulled down in 1972).

23. The Gatehouse, at the entrance to the Manor grounds, which stood nearly opposite the modern road island at the top of Grinstead Lane.

24. The original *Sussex Pad* Inn which was burnt down in 1905.

25. Lancing United F.C. 1921–22. *Back row l. to r.*: Bert Merriott; ? Burstowe; Joe Strotten; Len Lawrence; Alick Battrick; Ben Steer. *Middle row*: Bill Scrace; Fred Battrick; Fred Peters. *Bottom row*: Rupert Battrick; Buller Battrick; Gordon Barrett; Ted Edwards; Ted Munnery.

26. Culver House *c.* 1930, which stood near the south corner of Culver Road and North Road. The ~~parade~~ *site* is now covered by a parade of shops.

27. The old Posting House, once known as 'Walnut Tree Cottage', in Mill Road, North Lancing.

28. (*above*) The level-crossing gates, Lancing, *c.* 1906. The three children shown are, from left to right: Ralph Hildred and Ruby Piper.

29. A game of cricket outside the Lancing Grammar School. *c.* 18( This building later became 'The Chestnuts' Home of Rest. The site is now covered by the parade of shops known as Regent Buildings.

Fig. 16. Petrified Tree Stump—Old Salts Farm

After the formation of the original bank the river diverted its course from its main outfall near the extreme west of the farm to about its present outfall, this mainly owing to the obstruction caused by the bank. The river, still unconfined by banks, flooded the low-lying areas at times of high tide, leaving deposits of sand and mud over these areas. This process continued until some two hundred years ago when banks with a revetment of chalk were built along the sides of the river. The banks contained sluice gates to let storm-water escape into the river at low-tide. By the time the banks were formed, some four feet of sandy soil had been deposited over the sand and shingle washed in by the sea. During this century the original bank has been raised and strengthened by the sea defences work so arranged to trap shingle and widen the bank. The river banks have also been raised and revetted with blocks of chalk.

The confinement of the river led to slight flooding of the lowland during spring tides after heavy rainfall. To stop this the stream running across the farms and a proper outlet into the

river were so constructed as to confine water at high tide and
release it to the river at low tide. The flooding was practically
stopped, but at times there was slight flooding on an area called
Salt Lake, north-west of the farm, on which houses have now
been built. This flooding has stopped owing to the natural
erosion of the banks of the stream, which, together with proper
cleansing, has widened it sufficiently to take storm-water when
tide-bound, or during the severest rain.

In 1921 the Steyning West Rural District Council developed
a small housing estate named Wencelling Cottages on part of
New Salts Farm. This development was followed by specula-
tive building along the Brighton Road westwards to Lancing
village. There was very slight flooding in isolated spots, but it
was caused mainly by overflowing cesspools. This flooding
disappeared when sewers were laid some thirteen years later.

When sewers were made available for limited development,
plans were passed for the development of land north of the
Brighton Road known as the Hasler Estate. At this time there
was little that could be done to prevent the development or to
enforce proper drainage of the roads. Plans were, however,
passed subject to storm-water sewers being laid to discharge
into the stream. Much of this development was over the beds
of beach, and when soak-pits were dug to take away surface
water the reverse took place at high-tide, when water came out
of the gullies instead of running into them. The water went
down with the tide. This condition still exists and can be over-
come by draining into the stream. Development stopped when
war was declared. Anti-aircraft batteries and ammunition pits
were dug into the ground to the north of Hasler Estate, and
bombs were dropped which damaged the sewers, causing
leaks and overloaded sewage pumps.

After the war some development took place. Approximately
sixty houses were built on land which was part of New and
Old Salts Farms at the same ground level as the existing and
proposed houses.

Many houses have been built on the County Council's estate,
south of Brighton Road, on land which is lower than that of
the proposed estate. The land is of the same formation as the
Old Salts Farm, but with much more sand mixed with the soil.

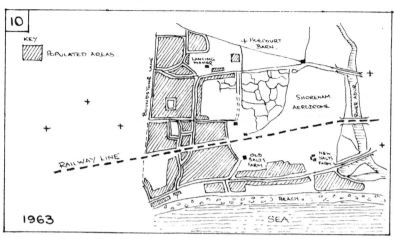

Diagram 10: Outline of the coast, 1963.

Diagram No. 10 shows the land as it was in 1963. It has changed very little since then.

The following lists show all the known owners and occupiers of the two farms.

**Old Salts Farm**

| Date | Owners | Occupier/Renter |
|---|---|---|
| 1684–1725 | Sir William Goring | December 1723, William Winton: |
| 1725–1780 | Charles Biddulph | lease for 21 years |
| 1780–1790 | Charles/John Biddulph | Richard Jay |
| 1791–1792 | John Biddulph | James Penfold |
| 1793–1797 | John Biddulph | James Penfold and Robert Holmes |
| 1798–1800 | John Biddulph | Robert Holmes (son of John) |
| 1801–1809 | John Biddulph | John Holmes |
| 1810–1827 | John Biddulph | Robert Holmes (son of John) |
| 1827–1828 | James Martin Lloyd | Robert Holmes (son of John) |
| 1829–1844 | James Martin Lloyd | Henry Botting |
| 1844–1855 | Rebecca/Elizabeth Lloyd and then G. K. Carr-Lloyd | Henry Botting |
| 1856–1858 | Rebecca/Elizabeth Lloyd and then G. K. Carr-Lloyd | |

*continued—*

| Date | Owners | Occupier/Renter |
|------|--------|-----------------|
| 1858–1873 | G. K. Carr-Lloyd | George Stanford |
| 1874–1877 | G. K. Carr-Lloyd | Fred Stanford |
| 1878–1907 | James Martin Carr-Lloyd | Thomas Watson |
| 1907–1978 | Members of the Easter family | (1909 Robert Lee) |

It is interesting to note that only four families have had connections with the ownership of the farm during its present 294 years' existence, as shown in the following summary:

| | |
|------|------|
| Goring family | 31 years |
| Biddulph family | 102 years |
| Lloyd and Carr-Lloyd family | 80 years |
| Easter family | 71 years (to 1978) |

**New Salts Farm**

| Date | Owners | Occupier/Renter |
|------|--------|-----------------|
| 1770–1780 | Charles Biddulph | |
| 1780–1785 | Charles/John Biddulph | John Weller |
| 1786–1818 | John Biddulph | John Grinstead |
| 1819–1820 | John Biddulph | Nathaniel Grinstead |
| 1821–1822 | John Biddulph | Nathanial Grinstead and Co. |
| 1823–1827 | John Biddulph | Edward Grinstead |
| 1827–1832 | James Martin Lloyd | Edward Grinstead |
| 1833–1837 | James Martin Lloyd | |
| 1838 | James Martin Lloyd | Will. Duke, Ann Harriett Duke and James Penfold |
| 1839–1854 | James/Rebecca/Elizabeth Lloyd and then G. K. Carr-Lloyd | |
| 1855–1868 | G. K. Carr-Lloyd | James Penfold |
| 1869–1872 | G. K. Carr-Lloyd | |
| 1873–1878 | G. K./J. M. Carr-Lloyd | Charles Duke |
| 1878 | J. M. Carr-Lloyd | Mrs. Wallace |
| 1879–1894 | J. M. Carr-Lloyd | |
| 1895 | J. M. Carr-Lloyd | Charles Bernard Duke |
| 1896–1898 | J. M. Carr-Lloyd | |
| 1899–1907 | J. M. Carr-Lloyd | Fred. Walter Trott |
| 1907–1912 | Members of the Easter family | Fred. Walter Trott |
| 1912–1978 | Ditto | |

For more than two hundred years the farm was owned by members of only three different families, as follows:

| | |
|---|---|
| Biddulph family | over 57 years |
| Lloyd and Carr-Lloyd family | 80 years |
| Easter family (present owners) | 71 years (to 1978) |

*Chapter Four*

## OLD BUILDINGS OF LANCING

FOR THE PURPOSE of identifying and recording the old buildings, three plans have been prepared based on the Tithe Map of Lancing of 1838. Each building or group of buildings has been given a number to which the notes refer. Many of these buildings have long since been demolished and are only identifiable from references contained in deeds or maps. However, a few pictures or sketches survive of the later or more picturesque buildings, but nothing like a full history of each building has been compiled. The available information has been collated and is contained in the following notes.

Fig. 17. Coastguard Cottages—South Lancing (No. 1)

## Section I

### 1. *Coastguard Cottages and Station*

The earliest known view of the coastguard station is shown in the *Worthing Map Story,* by Henfrey Smail, and is dated 1826. The Enclosure Map of 1803 for Lancing shows a plot of land allotted on which the station buildings were erected between 1803 and 1826. Originally the buildings stood on a fairly high point known as the Hurst Bank, now the Chester Avenue area. The bank dropped sharply to the Worthing–Shoreham coast road, and fields stretched out to the sea, which was much further to the south than it is today.

In 1838 the Tithe Award describes the property as a station house, cottages and garden being in the occupation of members of the Government and owned by Mary Latchford. In 1847 a will shows the house to be owned by Henrietta Latchford. From this point the ownership of the station buildings is difficult to trace until December 1939 when they were sold to West Sussex County Council. From information contained in the Worthing and District Local Directory of 1912 it appears that there were eight cottages at the front and some others at the rear which remained until they were finally demolished in the 1950s.

### 2. *Bank Cottage*

The name is derived from the steep bank which once existed to the south of the cottage. The cottage was built *c.* 1800, as the Overseers' Records for Lancing show in 1800 'Mr. Dabb's new House'. In 1838 a William Dabbs still occupied the premises while from at least 1866 until 1899 Henry Thomas Northcroft was the owner. In 1889 it was used as a convalescent home for people from the poverty-stricken East End of London. Most of the chosen few who used the cottage throughout the summer period looked upon the sea for the first time in their lives and enjoyed the benefits of the fresh air. These parties of sufferers were organised by William Chorley, who was a director of the North-East London Mission. Eventually the numbers of those who wished to use the home far outweighed those who could

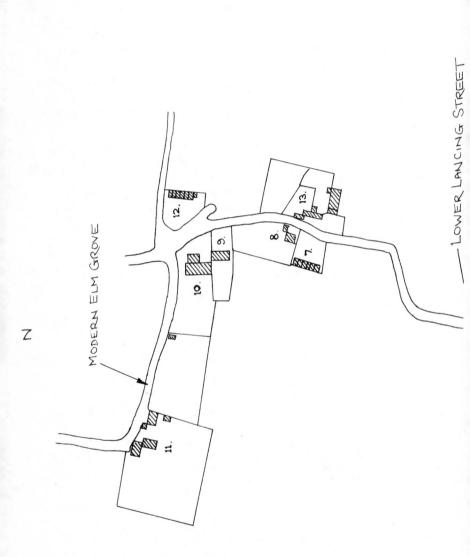

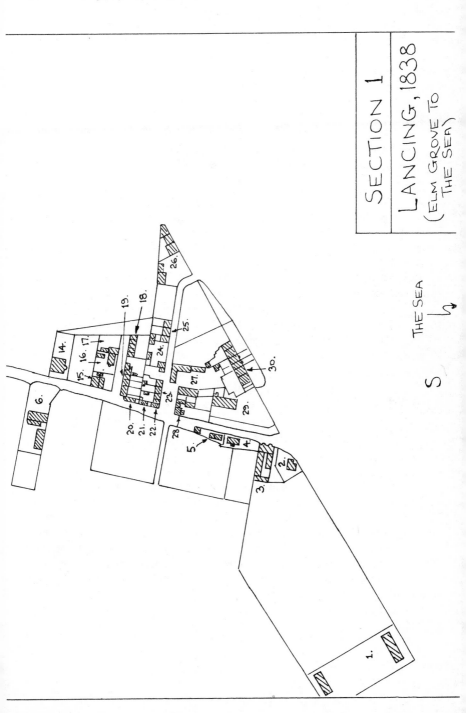

SECTION 1

LANCING, 1838

(ELM GROVE TO THE SEA)

adequately be accommodated, and Mr. Chorley had to search for a larger home. At present a red brick house still stands on the site with some of the old flint wall in front of the house remaining.

## 3. 'Horseshoes' Inn

The inn (now called the *Three Horseshoes*) was built in 1807 and the reason for the original name was not readily apparent until information from the Overseers' Records of Lancing showed that there was an even earlier building known as 'The Horseshoes' in 1789, occupied by a John Stone. Also mentioned is the 'Horseshoes' Croft'. As a croft is a small piece of land close to a house, it is not unreasonable to expect a building with the same name to be adjacent to the croft.

The Enclosure Map of Lancing for 1803 shows a piece of ground known as the Horsehoe field on the opposite side of the road to the modern inn in South Street, and now covered by Regent Buildings. The field, presumably so named because of its similarity to the shape of a horseshoe, had a small building on the north side next to the Street (now South Street). This building, identified as a cottage (see No. 22), was situated on the corner of East Street. An old photograph of the building shows its structure as being very similar to those of other buildings in Lancing known to have been built prior to 1780. On the back of this photograph was an interesting note which mentions that the cottage was once a smugglers' inn. This information from different sources suggests that this building was almost certainly the original *Horseshoes* inn.

By 1800 William Steel was occupier of the original inn and probably also the owner, for the Overseers' Records in 1807 show that a poor rate of £12 was levied on William Steele 'for the new Horshoes'. Previously it had been only £3 10s. 0d. for the original building. Steele may have been the owner of the new building as well. Later he must have fallen upon hard times, for on 13 April 1812 there was 'an assignment by William Steele, Innkeeper to James Newnum of Southwick, Brewer and James Penfold of Goring, farmer, of all his household furniture, chattels and stock-in trade etc. for the benefit of his creditors'. In 1813 a Mr. Patrick is named as the owner, while from 1821 to 1838 its owner is shown as Richard Tamplin, although William Steele remained as innkeeper throughout the entire period. Richard Tamplin was the fore-runner of Tamplin's Breweries, who still owned the inn more than a century later.

Old posters show that during the 1820s auctions of buildings and land were carried out in the inn, and one poster in par-ticular, dated 1821, quotes the name of the *Three Horseshoes* inn. The building still exists as a public house, in its original shape, but has, no doubt, had many renovations and repairs during the past 171 years.

Nearly two hundred years ago the original inn, then a small cottage, was the last building before the road reached the seashore, and, no doubt, was the Lancing fishermen's first refuge on their way back to the village after their fishing acti-vities. The inn was in a very lonely spot and one can imagine how easily it could have been frequented by smugglers. By the 1820s the coastguard station had been erected near the shore and probably helped to lessen the incidence of smuggling in Lancing, smuggling being rife all along the Sussex coast during this period. The known occupiers and owners of the *Horseshoe* inn up to 1931 are as follows:

|  | Date | Owner | Innkeeper |
|---|---|---|---|
| The original inn | 1789 |  | H. Hannington |
| The original inn | 1790–94 |  | J. Stone |
| The original inn | 1800–07 | W. Steele | William Steele |
| The 'modern' inn | 1807–12 | W. Steele | William Steele |
| The 'modern' inn | 1813 | Mr. Patrick | William Steele |
| The 'modern' inn | 1814–21 |  | William Steele |
| The 'modern' inn | 1821–38 | Richard Tamplin | William Steele |
| The 'modern' inn | 1855 | Tamplin family | William Whittle |
| The 'modern' inn | 1858 | Tamplin family | Robert Martin |
| The 'modern' inn | 1866–72 | Tamplin family | William Dowell |
| The 'modern' inn | 1873–78 | Tamplin family | George Henry Brewer |
| The 'modern' inn | 1878-1915 | Tamplin family | George N. Prideaux, sr. |
| The 'modern' inn | 1915-1931 |  | George N. Prideaux, jr. |

## 4. *Lorne Cottage*

Lorne Cottage stood next to and south of Hope Lodge in South Street and was a seven-roomed building. By 1838 there was a building on the site described as two cottages, owned and occupied by the landlord of the *Horseshoes* inn. It is not not known whether these two original cottages were made into one building or demolished and a new house built, but by 1878, at least, the name Lorne Cottage appeared.

In the spring of 1895 the cottage fell empty and by this time there were many appeals being made to the 'Homes of Rest' in Lancing (later to be known as the 'Southern Convalescent Homes Inc.') by the wives, mothers and sisters who were staying in the homes for their menfolk to share with them the benefits of Lancing air and the home's dietary. This inspired Mr. Chorley of the 'Homes of Rest' to utilise Lorne Cottage as a home for men.

The house was furnished to accommodate eight men, a matron and helper, and in June 1895 a dedicatory service, attended by several friends of the work from London, marked its opening. During its first year, as with several of the homes, it was found inadequate to meet the demands, and it was obvious that a larger house would be needed. This did not materialise for another three years and so the work went on at Lorne Cottage.

Many men who normally spent their short annual holiday in London parks were able to avail themselves of a holiday by the sea at a price within their reach, whilst convalescents discharged from London hospitals regained their normal strength in what seemed an incredibly short time. However, in 1898 the men moved to a larger house. The cottage then became an asylum for eight aged women who could no longer work and would otherwise be admitted to the dreaded workhouse. At the cottage at least a few of them could spend the remainder of their days in peace and comfort. This home was closed in 1907 when they moved to Mount Hermon, a house on the seafront road facing the sea.

Lorne Cottage was later occupied by the McCarthy family. Many of their postcards of old Lancing were sold from their shop on the corner of Roberts Road (the shop is at present

Fig. 18. Hope Lodge, South Lancing (No. 5)

known as 'Surfleets'). Lorne Cottage had disappeared by
1939 when Marine Buildings were erected on the site.

## 5. Cottage/Hope Lodge

Hope Lodge stood on a site in front of the modern Sunbeam
Memorial Home, and to the north of Lorne Cottage. The site
is now partly covered by the parade of shops known as Marine
Buildings.

Originally the ground was wasteland granted to 'Michael
Clear of Lancing and his heirs' in 1791 by the lord of the
manor. It measured 90ft., north to south, and 24ft., east
to west. Eventually in 1807 part of the land passed to Thomas
Smith, of Worthing, corn chandler.

By the time the land was sold to a certain G. D. Brightwell in 1833 there were two tenements on the site. In 1835 they were bought by Thomas Shearman, and in 1838 the Tithe Award confirms that the property, described as a cottage and a garden, was owned by Shearman, and was occupied by a Miss Moss. Sometime after this date Hope Lodge was built, for in 1856 a plan of the ground is shown in a deed and the name of Hope Lodge is used. Several pieces of garden were gradually added to the site over the next few years.

By 1894 the women's home in the old Grammar School (No. 29) was well under way, but one of the problems encountered was that mothers with babies could hardly be excluded, yet some of the other guests' comfort and rest were often impaired by the noise of the babies.

In 1894 Mr. Chorley was pleading for funds to build a new day-room for the convenience of mothers with infants. However, in 1895 Hope Lodge was put up for sale, and Mr. Chorley set to work to collect the purchase money of £425. Many friends came forward in response to his appeal, and within a year the purchase money was raised. In June 1896 the Home for Mothers and Infants was opened with a service of praise.

By 1911 it was felt that Hope Lodge was becoming inadequate for the needs of a dozen families of small children, as it was found that a mother was seldom content to take only one of her offspring. A new home was required, and in 1911 money was being collected to build it. However, Hope Lodge remained until additional land was purchased and the new Bell Memorial Home for Women, and the Sunbeam Home for Children were built at the rear of the site in 1928. Hope Lodge was then demolished. Initially the two homes were virtually run as separate units. However, during the war the Homes were first requisitioned by the Ministry of Health as an Emergency No. 2 Hospital, but were never used, and later by the War Department.

In 1940 the Sunbeam Home was hit by a bomb and partly destroyed. Fortunately it had been evacuated and there were no casualties. By 1950, however, enough money had been raised by grants and the sale of the remainder of their property to have the Sunbeam Home rebuilt. The two homes were then organised and run as one unit. In 1964 a sun-lounge was added to complete the buildings as they are at the present time. This combined building now represents the remaining interests in Lancing of the Southern Convalescent Homes apart from two minor buildings which are leased.

It is interesting to note that the work of the Homes began in 1889. This was the year in which William Chorley, whose work with the North-East London Mission (originally Kingsland Mission) showed him some of the misery and suffering endured by people in the London slums, was kindly offered the use of Bank Cottage for the summer months rent free by the owner, Mr. Northcroft, to provide holidays for these people. This offer was gladly accepted by Mr. Chorley, who was director of the North-East London Mission, and for a year the cottage was used by people convalescing. Eventually the need was greater than could adequately be provided, and Mr. Chorley was searching for a home large enough to suit the increasing demand. In 1890 the former Grammar School was obtained, and so started the era of the 'Chestnuts', or the 'Maria Wenman Home' as it was later named (see No. 29). Other houses used as homes of rest were Lorne Cottage, Hope Lodge, Beachville, Channel View, Mount Hermon, and finally the Sunbeam and Bell Memorial homes.

In 1922 the Homes were registered as an Incorporation with Mr. Chorley as its first chairman, while his two sons and a daughter all took an active part in the running of them. Just before World War II the Rev. Walter Spencer (Superintendent of the South London Mission) was appointed to the council of the Homes. Later in 1938 he was appointed chairman and continued for five years. The fine work which the Homes carry out is in itself enough to justify its place in a history of Lancing; but also during its 85 years of existence it has affected the development of several of Lancing's early buildings. It was only through the kind co-operation of Sister Ivy Baldock from the Southern Convalescent Homes that notes on several of the houses in South Lancing were completed.

## 6. South Place (see No. 14)

Fig. 19. Yew-tree Cottages, South Lancing, *c.* 1908 (No. 7)

## 7. Yew-tree Cottages

This group of six flint-built cottages was erected between 1795 and 1803 in South Street, opposite Goring House. Old photographs of these cottages show a large tree in the front which appears to be a yew, from which these cottages probably took their name (see chapter on Yew-tree Farm). The cottages remained for over a hundred and fifty years before they were severely damaged by fire and had to be demolished in the late 1950s.

## 8. Cherry-tree Cottage

This building, shown attached to a butcher's shop in 1912, was called 'Cherry-tree Cottage' when it was built between 1820 and 1838. In 1838 it was described as a cottage and garden of about a quarter of an acre, owned and occupied by John Parker. It was demolished several years ago along with the butcher's shop (Hodson's for many years).

### 9. Methodist Chapel

A nonconformist meeting place in South Lancing was mentioned in 1815 and 1833, and a new chapel was opened in 1865, presumably on the same site as that shown on the Ordnance Survey map of 1869. This chapel was replaced in 1905 by the modern stone building which cost approximately £1,800.

### 10. Barn Yard

The old barn and yard erected south of the junction of the present Elm Grove and South Street were part of James Martin Lloyd's land in 1803 and remained so for many years. Eventually the site contained glasshouses and other outbuildings, being part of a market garden. These buildings were later demolished and a petrol station now stands on part of the site.

### 11. The Finches

In 1803 this site, at the end of Elm Grove on the south side, was referred to as Finches copyhold. In 1838 it was a dwelling house, barn and garden with a field adjoining, owned by John Harmer and occupied by Elizabeth Walls. Later in 1912 the house was called 'The Finches' and occupied by George Lisher, coal merchant and dairyman. A house with the same name still exists on the site.

Fig. 20. Exterior of Pond Row Cottages (No. 12)

### 12. Pond Row

These six cottages took their name from the pond that originally existed on the site, at the side of South Street, just south of the junction with the present King's Road. They were built between 1820 and 1838 and existed well into the 20th century before being demolished in the late 1950s.

## 13. Yew-tree Farm/Goring House (see Chapter Two)

## 14. South House and South Place

South House, in South Street, once described as a 'gaunt old house', was demolished in December 1937. On its site now stands the parade of shops and flats known as Lincoln Court. An article dated 4 December 1937 from the *Worthing Herald* informs us that the house was reputed to be about three hundred years old. However, Yeakell and Gardner's survey of Sussex in 1778 shows no sign of a house, but opposite was a yard and barn known as South Place. In 1782 the site of the house and South Place were part of Jeremiah Wackford's land. Mr. Wackford died in 1790 and the land was purchased by J. Foster, who appears to have built South House in about 1795, possibly on the site of an earlier house. The Church-wardens' accounts for 1796 show 'Mr. Foster's new House'. In 1800 the house is referred to as South House and this is one of the earliest mentions of the name so far found.

A counterpart of a lease in 1816 describes South Place as a 'barn, yard, milk-house, hovel and cowhouses belonging and the use of the road from Lancing Street through the yard and premises'. In 1851 the house was used as a dance school with seven girl pupils.[1]

For many years South House was used as a farmhouse, and during the First World War German prisoners were interned there. German coins were found on the premises by a subsequent owner. It has also been suggested that the house was haunted and that a secret passage existed. However, the author of the newspaper article previously mentioned decided to find out for himself. The following extract from the article shows the results of the investigation.

> One night this week (December 1937) we went over the place from top to bottom. Apart from cellars, two staircases—one of which rises from the kitchen to the roof almost like a ladder—and the eerie attics, we found nothing to 'write home about'.

Soon after this article was written the house was demolished, having stood for over a hundred and forty years.

The known occupiers are as follows:

| Date | Occupiers |
|------|-----------|
| 1796–1801 | J. Foster |
| 1802–1819 | Mrs. Jane Jamison |
| 1820–1828 | Charles Jamison |
| 1829–1836 | Elizabeth Staley |
| 1837–1847 | Maurice Jones |
| 1848–1849 | Edward Langford |
| 1851–1873 | Charles Bushby |

## Nos. 15–25 Inclusive

The remainder of the buildings in this section were built on land which forms part of an old enclosure dating from the 16th century, known as Blackman's Breach. This stretched from the site of South House to the modern lower Brighton Road. For the purpose of description it can be divided into three convenient pieces.

(a) Land immediately to the south of South House containing approximately a quarter of an acre which in 1804–5 was allocated to the Headborough of Lancing, G. Bushby. Part of this has been preserved and is used by the public as a garden (Headborough Gardens).

(b) The next piece of land is that occupied by Alma Street with the buildings and gardens either side. Under the Enclosures Act this land was allotted to John Moffatt and contained approximately half an acre. This land passed to Thomas Midmore, bricklayer, in 1808. Between then and 1838 the land was split into small parcels each large enough to contain a house. Alma Street was formed and buildings erected (Nos. 15–19 inclusive). A shop on the north-west corner of Alma Street was built later in 1855 and still exists today. For many years it was Trevett's sweetshop and continued in business as such into the 1950s.

(c) The third piece of land, known as the 'Horseshoe' field, was originally copyhold and descended in the Blackman family of Lancing during the 17th century. The next mention of this piece of land occurs in the 18th century when 'Old William

Swift' stated that he knew William Spicer (died in 1777), the owner of property called Blackman's Breach, who was the only son of Mary Spicer. When William Spicer died in 1777 he left a widow, Ann, and sons. The youngest son, John, took possession of the property by custom of the Manor. William Spicer had been Steward of the Manor and was probably the younger son of Joseph Spicer, who was Bailiff of the Manor in 1711, and had himself inherited the land by custom of the Manor. Apparently the land passed from John Spicer to Mr. Holmes and later it was purchased by James Stubbs. Eventually this land was sold to the Lancing Building Society and from this point on the land was divided into various pieces and buildings were erected, many of them (if not all) being controlled by this Society.

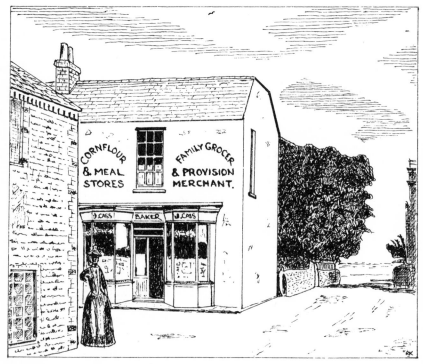

Fig. 21. The shop which later became 'Potter Bailey'. It was demolished in 1964. (Based on a photograph, *c.* 1900)

By 1838 East Street had been formed and Ivy Cottage, Colepen House and Seaview Cottages were already in existence, together with the shop later to become Potter Bailey's on the south-west corner of East Street. Potter Bailey sold their shop in 1963 and when it was demolished a few years ago it had been 'A. J. Smith, grocer and provisions'. The site was redeveloped in 1974-5 and now modern shops are on the site.

### 26. *Stork's Nest/Channel View* (near the eastern end of the Terrace and the lower Brighton Road, facing the sea.)

The original house was built *c*. 1820 and in 1838 was described as 'house, stables, barns and yard', owned and occupied by James Ireland. By at least 1866 it was named the 'Stork's Nest'. In 1898 the property came up for sale. Some of the property was sold off separately and the price eventually came within the region of practibility for the Southern Convalescent Homes. The offer of a year's lease while the money was being raised was gratefully accepted, and so in 1899 'Channel View' became a convalescent home for men. There was accommodation for 30 men and youths, more than three times the number that could be received at Lorne Cottage in South Street. However, three years after opening Channel View more room was needed, and an extension was decided upon. The framework of buildings at the rear of the house, formerly a coach-house and stables, was utilised to provide a dining-room on the ground floor and bedrooms above. Further accommodation for an additional 20 patients was also provided. By 1908 yet more room was required, and an iron bungalow was erected in the grounds, which gave an extra day-room for the younger men, and more bedrooms. This extended the home's maximum accommodation to sixty. This house still stands, and is known as Sussex Lodge.

### 27. *Coach House, Stable and Ground*

Very few details are known about this property except that in 1838 it was described as a 'Coach-house, stable and ground' owned and occupied by Captain Henry Forbes. It was most likely connected with the house and garden at the western end of the Terrace which was owned by the same person.

## 28. Grocer's Shop/Potter Bailey (see No. 25)

## 29. Lancing Grammar School/The Chestnuts

This house was built *c.* 1820 and in 1838 was described as a house, garden and yard owned and occupied by Maurice Jones. The house became Lancing Grammar School, and Maurice Jones was headmaster. Maurice Jones died on 5 December 1843, and left the property to his widow, Emma, and son, John Maurice Jones, also a schoolmaster, who moved to London.[2] According to a later legal statement made by his son, Maurice Jones had been in possession of the building for at least ten years before his death.

Later the property was mortgaged, and in 1845 Robert Wright became tenant, renting the buildings and ground. He was aged 27 and came to Lancing from Highgate School, London, where he had been a master for about five years. The 1851 Census returns in the Public Records Office yield the following information on the school: no street or road name was given, but the house was numbered 22. The residents in the house on the night of the census consisted of Robert Wright, his wife Ann and son Herbert, aged two, Joseph De la Rue, aged 25, assistant schoolmaster; one cook; two housemaids; one nurse; and 33 scholars.

In 1854 all the buildings, etc., were purchased by Robert Wright. However, he died in 1862 and left his property to his widow Ann. In 1863 Ann Wright married a William Parkins and moved to London. It seems, however, that she retained possession of the property until her death in 1891 and had let it to various tenants. Robert Wright had been a very keen photographer and some of the earliest known photographs of Lancing were taken by him, *c.* 1857.

William Washington Pyne became the next headmaster, and *Sussex Directories* show him to have been there in 1866 and 1879. He lived in Hope Lodge in 1878. In 1883 Robert

McEwan, a schoolmaster, of Richmond in Surrey, brother-in-law of Robert Wright, was described as a tenant in a counterpart of a lease. There is no evidence that he left Surrey, although a son of his, Albert McEwan, who went into the Navy is described at the time of his marriage as 'of Lancing'. When Ann Parkin (Robert Wright's widow) died in 1891 her son Herbert Edward Wright and Nicholas McEwan were the executors of her will. By the early part of 1890 the school had closed and the building was put up for sale.

The remainder of the story of the house is contained in a pamphlet dated 1911 which commemorates 'The coming of age of the Southern Convalescent Homes of Rest'. Mr. Chorley from the Homes of Rest heard of the subsequent purchase of the house and approached the purchaser, Mr. Wenman, who, in fact, expressed his willingness for the house to be used as a Home of Rest. The owner was already so impressed with Mr. Chorley's work at Bank Cottage that he offered a free lease of the building for 21 years if Mr. Chorley would use it in this way. Although this kind offer meant shouldering a great more responsibility it was gratefully accepted. The house was furnished and opened as the 'Maria Wenman Home of Rest', the name given it in memory of the owner's deceased wife to whose means the home owed its existence.

The former classrooms were converted into bedrooms or sitting-rooms, while the rest formed a spacious and lofty kitchen. For some time remnants of the old school remained in the form of maps which still adorned the walls. However, in time these too vanished and many of those who stayed in the home had no notion of the building's former use.

Within four months of opening the home had received over four hundred and fifty patients for varying lengths of time. A slight charge was then made in admission, for while numbers of patients were still admitted free of all cost, a charge was made according to the circumstances of the applicant, although these charges did not cover the complete cost.

By 1892 additions had been made to the accommodation which meant that 80 visitors could be received at one time, about half of them children. In 1893 the free lease of the house was withdrawn and the future looked very bleak.

However, the freehold of the property was offered to the Mission Trustees on very advantageous terms, although it still meant borrowing £900 to complete the deal. The deal went through and the Mission had their own home.

By 1900 many of the old school buildings were in a very bad state. Floors gave way and ceilings fell in. The old building known as the 'cottage' with 10 low-ceilinged rooms in two floors was completely inadequate. It was remodelled as a three-storey building of handsome appearance with airy bay windows. The 10 rooms were replaced with 14 spacious and well-lit bedrooms. The patients' sitting-room was enlarged and made more cheerful, and by 1901 a new wing had been added. By this time the old building was scarcely recognisable.

Up to 1902 the dining-hall of the home was a chapel for all four homes then in existence. This proved inadequate and inconvenient. Then a generous sympathiser of the work of Mr. Chorley, seeing the need for a mission room, gave £400 for this purpose and a new room was built above the dining-hall, seating more than a hundred patients.

The work carried on for many more years in the home, which was also later known as the Chestnuts and the Alexandra Home for Women. The buildings were finally demolished in the 1930s and the site is now partly covered by Regent Buildings. All the patients for the Southern Convalescent Homes are now catered for in the Sunbeam and Bell Memorial Homes which are situated almost opposite the site of the old Chestnuts home in South Street.

### 30. The Terrace

This row of terraced houses facing the sea contains one of the most interesting buildings in the area, namely Jubilee House. The building of this house was paid for by the Lancing Building Society. It was sold in 1822 by auction in the *Three Horseshoes* inn, and the poster[3] advertising the auction gives this interesting description of the house:

> Lot. 1. All that well known and newly erected freehold dwelling house with BOW WINDOW FRONT called the JUBILEE HOUSE, adjoining a dwelling house of Sir Everard Hume being on the Terrace

at South Lancing in a most eligible situation from the sea. The house which is substantially well built on the most approved plan comprises—in the basement, a servants' hall, capital cooking kitchen, Pantry and other convenient offices—on the ground floor a commodious Dining Parlour—on the first floor an excellent Drawing Room, 21ft. x 15ft. 6ins., with best Bed-room behind. On the second floor—three well proportioned Bed-rooms and on the third floor, three Bed-rooms. There is a good yard behind the house and a pump with excellent water.

The premises are in complete repair, fitted up in superior style and well furnished, fit for the immediate reception of a family of distinction.

The situation as a marine residence is delightful, within a short walk of Worthing, and eleven miles from Brighton, commanding an uninterrupted view of the surrounding country, the Sea, Brighton, Beachy Head, Worthing, the Isle of Wight etc. The London, Southampton, Chichester, Brighton and Worthing Coaches pass within a few yards of the house daily.

The Furniture may be taken at a fair valuation, or not, at the option of the purchaser.

From the accounts of the Society in 1822 it is established that the house was eventually sold for £625, but the purchaser is not mentioned.

Part of the terrace still exists, but has been modernised.

## Section 2

### 31. *Two Houses and Garden*

Very little is known about the two early houses shown on the 1838 map except that at the turn of this century an old photograph shows them as flint-built. They were demolished in about 1926 and two more houses were built on the same site. These later buildings had a thatched roof and were demolished in 1974. Shops now stand on the site.

### 32. *Cottage and Garden*

This cottage is shown on the map of 1770 and in 1838 was owned and occupied by John Terry. The cottage was demolished to make way for the railway, *c.* 1842.

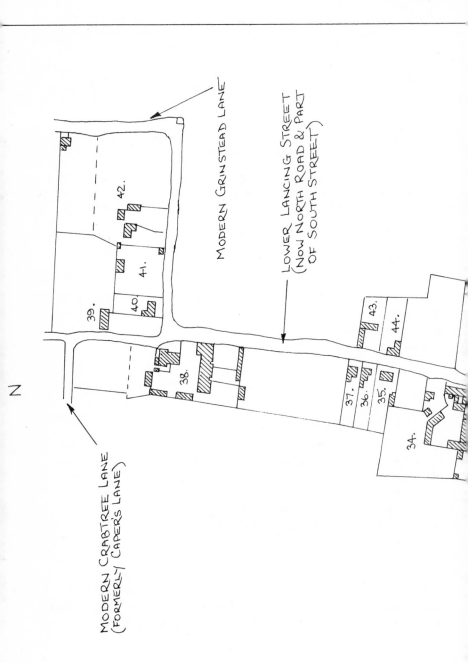

SECTION 2

LANCING, 1838

(CRABTREE LANE TO ELM GROVE)

APPROXIMATE POSITION OF RAILWAY.

MODERN ELM GROVE

Fig. 22. Old Cottages, South Lancing (No. 31)

### 33. Farmhouse, Buildings and Orchard

A small building is shown on the 1770 map and in 1803 other buildings appear. In 1838 it was owned by Robert Holmes. The buildings were demolished soon after the introduction of the railway in Lancing, when the *Railway* hotel and adjacent buildings to the north were erected.

### 34. Culverhouse Farm (see Chapter Two)

### 35. House and Garden/Gents Cottages

A building is shown in 1770 on the same site as the later building known as Gents Cottage in 1912. Without knowing what the original building was, it is impossible to say whether this building was added to and modernised to become Gents Cottage, or demolished and the new cottage built. Gents Cottage was eventually demolished and on the site is now a modern parade of shops.

### 36 and 37. Houses and Gardens

Both these houses were erected between 1820 and 1838 and were later known as Laurel Lodge and Myrtle Lodge respectively. These buildings were demolished in 1960.

### 38. Monk's Farm (see Chapter Two)

### 39. Barn and Yard

An ancient barn (built prior to 1770), only recently demolished in 1973. In 1803 the area was described as 'an old, inclosed rick yard belonging to J. Lloyd'.

Fig. 23. Monk's Farm Cottages and old barn (Nos. 39 and 40)

### 40. Monk's Farm Cottages

This block of three old flint cottages was built before 1770 and stood for about a hundred and fifty years before being demolished to make way for modern development.

### 41. House and Garden

This cottage was built *c.* 1780 and was originally owned by Bysshe Shelley. It descended through the Shelley family, and in 1838 was owned by Sir Timothy Shelley. Throughout most of this period it had been occupied by a member of the Swift family of Lancing. The name of Swift has been associated with Lancing for nearly seven hundred years. By 1912 the cottage was apparently known as 'Montague Cottage'. The building was demolished sometime in the 1920s, for in 1931 the Ordnance Survey maps show no sign of it.

## 42. Farmhouse, Barn, Yard and Garden

The farmhouse was erected before 1770. In 1912 it was known as 'Warrenhurst' and was a market garden. The site is now covered in part by houses and the other part by the *Britannia* public house.

## 43. Barn, Hovel and Yard

In 1748 this site formed part of 16 acres of freehold land belonging to Edward Soutton, farmer of Lancing, and was known as a hemp plot. Around 1775 a messuage and stable were erected on the site. By 1801, however, a deed shows that the messuage, cottage or tenement was intended to be converted into a barn, close and hovel. At this time it was owned by Mary and Richard Dyer. In 1838 it appears that the intention had been carried out, for the site and buildings were described as a barn, hovel and yard and known as 'Late Dyers' owned by James Martin Lloyd.

The position of the site can be approximately located as the junction of North Farm Road and North Road. The old buildings were probably demolished when North Farm Road was formed in the 1930s.

## 44. Three Houses and Garden

This old block of three tenements was built prior to 1770 and still remained in 1931. The buildings were situated to the north of the old Almshouses in Lancing and just south of the junction of North Farm Road and North Road. In 1922 these buildings were described as flint-built with thatched roofs, each containing two bedrooms, a living room and a scullery. They all shared a washhouse, and were numbered 33–35 North Road. They have now gone and flats stand on the site.

### 45. House, Barn and Yard

No other details of these buildings are known except that they were built between 1778 and 1803. Between 1869 and 1899 they were demolished and replaced by Littlecroft Cottages, which in turn have been replaced by a small parade of shops.

### 46. Four Cottages under one roof

These cottages were erected between 1803 and 1838. Later the northernmost one was called Ivy Cottage, and the remainder became shops.

### 47. House and Garden/Rose Cottage

This building can be traced back to 1640 when the site was described as having a house, barn and orchard situated in 'South Lansinge', with one acre of land lying to the east.

The property was owned by a Robert Westredge, a yeoman. After many different owners the property was secured by Thomas Dyer in 1776. By 1838 it was owned by Charles Caplin and described as a house and garden. It appears that later the name of the house was Rose Cottage. The house no longer exists and has a modern building on its site.

### 48. Garden Ground and Stable.

The stable stood adjacent to the present King's Road. By 1899 it appears to have been integrated into the buildings belonging to a nursery on the site.

**Section 3**

Fig. 24. The Corner House (No. 49) and the Old Cottage (No. 59),
North Lancing

### 49. *The Corner House (now the 'Sussex Potter')*

The building on the site at present was built in the 1930s.
Originally an old house stood on the corner of Manor Road,
near the junction with Mill Road and almost exactly opposite
the old thatched cottage. It was named aptly enough the
Corner House. This name was later used by the modern public
house before being renamed the *Sussex Potter* in recent years.

The old house was built before 1770. In the latter part of the
18th century it was known as 'Mr. Bishop's House' and was
occupied by William Allin. During the 19th century it was
used as a shop, and in 1838 was described as a 'house, shop,
stable and garden'. In 1911 it was sold to the Lloyd family
and was known as 'East Lane House', no doubt due to its
situation at the north end of the old East Laine Field. The
Worthing and District *Directory* for 1927 shows the name
'Corner House' being used some time before it was demolished.

The early known occupiers of the original building were:

| | |
|---|---|
| Before 1780 | Mr. Bishop |
| 1780–1827 | William Allin |
| 1828–1830 | William Tynell |
| 1831–1832 | E. B. Parkhurst |
| 1838 | Thomas Allin |
| 1911 | J. M. Carr-Lloyd (owner) |

## 50 Friar's Acre/Brickhouse Farm (see Chapter Two)

Fig. 25. Church Farm Cottages and North Lancing Church (from the west)

## 51. The Parish Church and Vicarage

The Domesday Book does not mention a church in Lancing, and from remains of Norman work in the chancel it appears that the North Lancing parish church was built early in the 12th century. In the latter part of the 13th century the church was rebuilt. There were then alterations to the tower, and a low

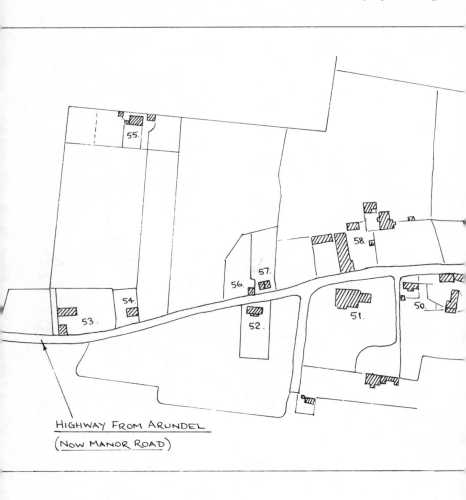

HIGHWAY FROM ARUNDEL
(NOW MANOR ROAD)

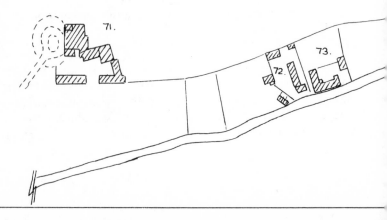

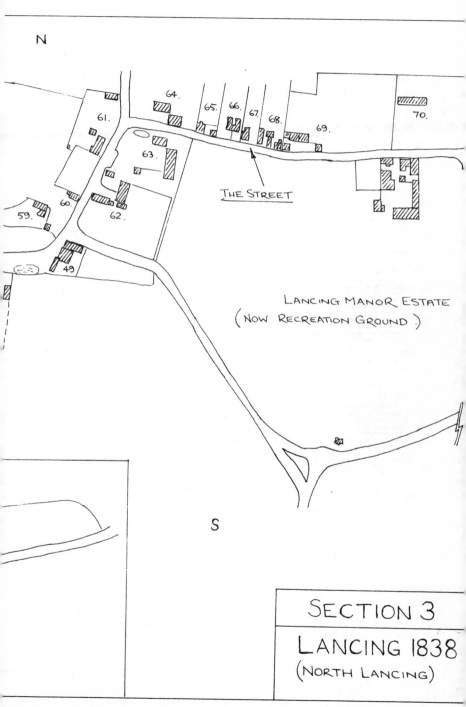

N

64.
65. 66. 67. 68.
69.
70.
61.
63.
60.
59.
62.
49.

THE STREET

LANCING MANOR ESTATE
( NOW RECREATION GROUND )

S

SECTION 3

LANCING 1838
(NORTH LANCING)

roof was added in 1618. However, it was allowed to deteriorate until 1827, when, according to the historian Cartwright, 'the church has been put into a state of complete repair; the deformities of whitewash have been removed, some new windows have been added, and the whole restored with much good taste, and with a due regard to the accommodation and convenience of the parishioners. These improvements have been carried on under the inspection, and chiefly at the expense of the present vicar [Rev. Thomas Nash]'.

Churchwardens' presentments for Lancing during the 17th century show that in 1626 'our church and tower was fallen downe and hath bin a building uppe these many years, and is not as yet finished; but is likely to fall down agayne'. This does seem to indicate that the alterations of 1618 may have been necessary because the tower and church had collapsed! During the 17th century it appears that the church was very much in decay, and there were many instances of people not having paid their tax for church repairs.

In 1624 the minister, Thomas Robinson, upset his parishioners when, instead of building a sorely-needed barn in the vicarage grounds, he built a cottage at the back of the vicarage and put a tenant in it. Later it was stated that because of the felling of trees in the churchyard, the walls were beaten down and the churchyard filled with saw-pits, logs and trees, 'so as it lieth more like a wood yard than a churchyard—most unseemly'.

In 1963 the church (which is generally accepted as being dedicated to St. James-the-Less) was again redecorated and restored. The exterior of the church is constructed mainly of dressed flint. Only the south porch and possibly the west doorway are relics of the original church. Inside is a canopied recess which covers a stone coffin. It is thought that it is the tomb of Michael de Poynings who bestowed the advowsons and rectorial tithes of the church to the small priory of Mottenden in Kent in 1350.

It is impossible to say how many vicarage buildings there have been on the same site, but the Church Building Papers of 1817 show that plans were presented by Nathaniel Ponder for a new building. The old building was subsequently knocked down except for the main doorway, the north wall (to a height of seven feet) and two new rooms to the south. The cost of the old materials was estimated at £300; the building of the vicarage was then finished for £650. This building appears to have been the one pulled down in 1933. The present vicarage stands on the same site.

## 52. *Two Tenements*

Although a building is shown on this site in 1770 it would appear that it was an earlier tenement or barn, for the record of the poor relief for Lancing indicates that the building shown on the 1838 map was erected *c.* 1799. By 1803 it was shown as belonging to Stubbs and remained so until at least 1814. According to the Ordnance Survey maps at some time between 1869 and 1899 the house was demolished and a glasshouse erected on the site. By 1942 the plot was empty, but now the site has again been built upon.

The known occupiers and owners are as follows:

|  | Occupiers | Owner |
|---|---|---|
| 1799–1814 | Thomas Saunders | M. Stubbs |
| 1838 | Mrs. Saunders | M. Stubbs |
|  | George Grover |  |

## 53. *House, Stable and Garden (Old Walls)*

By 1838 this site had two separate buildings on it. The building to the north was a cottage, and the other, near the road, was a stable.

The cottage is shown on the 1770 map of Lancing and was probably built *c.* 1750. In 1803 the cottage was owned by a person named Marshall, according to the 1803 Enclosure Map of Lancing, and later it became a gardener's cottage for the the Fircroft estate (see No. 55). A tarmacadam road was laid to the west of the cottage leading to Fircroft and a recent extension built on the western end of the cottage uncovered part of the road. The name of the old cottage was 'West

Fig. 26. Old Walls, North Lancing (No. 53), formerly West Cottage

Cottage' before it was changed to its present one of Old Walls. The old name was no doubt due to its originally being the most westerly building in North Lancing.

The building shown adjacent to the road was originally a stable and was built between 1803 and 1838. For many years it remained a stable until early this century when it was converted into classrooms for the owner of the cottage, who was a school teacher. About sixteen years ago the building was converted into a private house and sold independently of the cottage. Now it has only a historical connection with the original cottage.

### 54. House and Garden (Willow Cottage)

This old house is shown on the map of 1770. Its present name, Willow Cottage, is derived from a willow tree which

Fig. 27. Willow Cottage, North Lancing (No. 54).

once grew on the west side of the building. This tree was cut down a few years ago due to its dangerous condition.

Although according to the Tithe Award of 1838 the property was described as a house and garden, it must have been two cottages at some stage, because it shows definite signs of having been converted into one cottage from two. (It was possibly an original house divided into two cottages after 1838, and later converted back to one after 1912, as the Ordnance Survey map for that year shows it divided). The outside of the building, at the rear, shows signs of having had two distinct doorways, and the interior indicates that it was a pair of 'two up and two down' cottages. Its earlier name of 'Glebe Cottages' certainly suggests more than one.

An old stable exists on the west side of the house abutting the road. It has now been converted into a garage and was originally built sometime between 1838 and 1869. In the narrow front garden is an old pump which is situated in a well approximately sixty feet deep. The well is in a good state of preservation and still contains water, but is covered over for safety reasons.

In 1838 the owner-occupier was Stephen Grover, and in *Kelly's Directories* for Sussex, 1855-1878, are mentions of someone of the same name described as a market gardener. Ordnance Survey maps between 1869 and 1942 show the existence of glasshouses surrounding the walled garden and, at one stage, there were two glasshouses inside the garden against the old flint walls. These two glasshouses no longer exist, while the decline of the market garden industry and modern building development have been responsible for the removal of the others.

### 55. Fircroft

The original house (later known as Fir Cottage and finally Fircroft) was built in 1801 for a Mr. Miller. The 1869 map shows it as Fir Cottage, whilst in 1878 it became Fir-Croft. This name continued into the 1930s when it eventually became *Fircroft* private hotel. Eventually it was demolished and the name survives in Fircroft Avenue.

The early known owners and occupiers were:

|           | Owner                | Occupier             | Name        |
| --------- | -------------------- | -------------------- | ----------- |
| 1801–1821 | Mr. and Mrs. Miller  | Mr. and Mrs. Miller  |             |
| 1822      | Mrs. Miller          | Mrs. Miller          |             |
| 1838      | Mary Miller          | Charles Sunderland   |             |
| 1866      |                      | Mrs. Raymont         | Fir Cottage |
| 1872–90   |                      | Richard Came         | Fir Croft   |

### 56. Two Tenements

In 1770 the area on which these two tenements (and also those described in 57) were built is shown as one piece of land. In 1770 there was a building on this site in a similar position to that shown as No. 56 on the map. In 1803 it was owned by Carver, whilst in 1838 the building was described as two tenements owned and occupied by J. Lishner. The building was eventually bought by the Lloyd family on 28 July 1863 from a person named Ellis for £210. The building is shown on the 1942 Ordnance Survey map. It was eventually named 'Honeysuckle Cottage' and demolished when the road known as Green Oaks was formed.

### 57. Two Tenements

These two tenements were built between 1803 and 1838 when they were owned by M. Stubbs. During the latter part of the 19th century they were demolished and the house, at one time called 'Fairview', and at present known as the 'Red House', was built on the site.

### 58. North Farm/Church Farm (see also Chapter Two)

The cottages on this site dated at least from the 18th century and were at right-angles to the road, exactly opposite the church. In 1922 they were described as 'Two flint built and slate roofed cottages, each containing three Bedrooms, Kitchen, Lobby and Scullery. Outside W.C.'s'. Other property was mentioned as follows: 'Large flint built and slate roofed Barn, 5-stall Carthorse Stable, open yard with Hovel'.

The cottages no longer exist. It has been suggested that they were demolished in connection with widening the Manor Road. Although the 1942 Ordnance Survey map shows the site to be covered by houses belonging to Fircroft Avenue.

### 59. House/Old Thatched Cottage

The cottage is almost certainly the oldest surviving building in North Lancing; one part of its north side is reputed to be 15th-century, The rest was probably burnt or destroyed and rebuilt in the early 17th century.

This cottage, being so old, has several tales attached to it which cannot be substantiated. An example is that some of the beams in the cottage came from Spanish galleons which were battered off the coast near Rye at the time of the Armada.

Fig. 28. Old Cottage, Mill Road, *c.* 1900 (No. 59)

These beams may have come from ships washed up at Lancing, but it is unlikely that they came from the Armada.

More examples are shown in the following extract from a newspaper report of 27 November 1935:

> Situated on what was in those days the main highway, the Cottage has been visited by many kings and queens who passed it on their way to Portsmouth. Queen Elizabeth, it is said, stayed there while her palfrey was shod at the village forge nearby. James II stayed on his way to Shoreham to take ship for France.

The cottage was certainly situated on the main highway in those days, but the other statements seem to be purely conjecture. The evidence of a passage at the side of the house which led to an oven at the rear of the building and the direct route to the mill from the house seems to indicate that this may have been the village bakery at one time.

*60 National School House/Church of England School.*

In 1811 a society was founded and known as 'The National Society for the education of the poor in the Principles of the

Fig. 29. Church of England School, North Lancing (No. 60)

Established Church'. Day-schools were provided by the Society and Anglican instruction was given, combined with the adoption of the monitorial system devised by Andrew Bell (1753–1832). This system of instruction entailed the elder boys or monitors taking charge of the rest and giving instruction under the supervision of the teachers.[4]

In 1838 the Tithe Map of Lancing shows that a National School had been erected on the present site of the North Lancing School. It had , in fact, been erected in 1826. This early building was slightly further to the north of the present building and adjacent to Mill Road.

There is little doubt that the National School in North Lancing was soon in difficulties due to lack of space, for a drawing of 1871 shows that an extension had been built northwards on the east end of the school.[5] The attendance had risen from 38 pupils in 1833 to 65 pupils by 1847. Plans were submitted in 1871 by an architect, Richard Came, who lived at Fircroft in Lancing, for a new Church of England school, and these were passed, except for a few minor changes. The *Post Office Directory* of 1890 shows that the new school was erected in 1872 at a cost of £900, raised by subscription. This school consisted of one large central room, divided into two by a curtain, an infants' room at the western end of the building, and a residence for the schoolmistress at the eastern end.

It is quite probable that the Elementary Education Act of 1870 helped to decide that a new school was required in Lancing. This Act provided that school boards were to be elected with powers to establish and maintain elementary schools by levying rates, charging fees and receiving government grants. The boards could also make bye-laws compelling children between the ages of five and twelve to attend school.[4] Originally the children paid 2d. each to attend.

The new school was opened on 16 September 1872 by Miss Emma Parker,[6] a certificated teached trained at Brighton College, with Miss Charlotte Tate in charge of the infants' department. Initially 87 children were admitted to the school, 57 in the upper and 30 in the infants'.

An extract from the old school log-book indicates the educational problems of the new school.[6]

> September, 18th, 1872. The children are exceedingly backward in Arithmetic and Writing with the exception of a few of the eldest girls who can do a simple Addition sum, while a large proportion of them cannot even make the figures.

By 4 October 1872 there were 99 children at the school and there are several instances in the log-book of the school attendance being low due to the weather and the distance that some of the children had to travel. There are other references showing how different schools were over a century ago:

> 1874, Friday, July 24th. The average is low for this week so many children are at work in the fields. Break up this morning for the Harvest holiday.

> 1876. A..... B..... has left because his mother cannot afford to pay the extra 2d. per week.

It would appear from the previous references that compulsory attendance at the Lancing school was either not introduced or not enforced. However, the Education Act of 1880 supplemented the 1870 Act and made school attendance up to the age of 10 years compulsory. A certificate could be obtained when the age of 10 was reached, provided that enough attendances had been registered. Otherwise the pupil had to carry on to the age of thirteen.

By 1893 the average attendance was 147;[7] by 1897 the school was full and the inspector's report for the year indicates the need for a new classroom. This had been accomplished by 1912, for the Ordnance Survey map of that year shows a new classroom on the south of the building and the infants' room extending to the north wall. Extra toilets and a few other innovations were added.

In 1902 a further Education Act allowed for financial aid from the local authorities and by 1905 the average attendance had grown to one hundred and seventy. In 1936 plans were drawn up by the West Sussex County Council for new additions to the school, and a new junior and infants' school was opened at North Lancing in 1940. The 1942 Ordnance Survey map shows new buildings in the field to the west of the school.

The Education Act of 1944 reduced the number of education authorities by making the County and County Borough Councils responsible for local education. The Board of Education became the Department of Education and established universal free secondary education. In 1975 the schools in the parish were reorganised, and North Lancing became a combined first and middle school.[8]

The Victorian part of the old school is still in use and appears very similar to earlier views of the school, although the surrounding area has altered.

### 61. House (Old Posting House) (see Chapter two, p. 45)

Although this house still exists and is obviously old, very few details are known about it. Although the house is believed to have been built *c.* 1540, it is not shown on the map of 1770 because the map was originally drawn to show all the property of the lord of the manor, and this particular house did not belong to him. In 1838 it was described only as a house, and it was not until 1869 that the house was shown as North Lancing Post Office. It is certain that this was the early posting house where mail was delivered and collected, and no doubt horses and passengers rested, while, in the old smithy opposite, the

Fig. 30. The Old Posting House, Mill Road, North Lancing, *c.* 1939

Fig. 31. Old Barn in Mill Road, now converted into a house known as Barn Elms. Originally standing on land belonging to the Posting House

horses' shoes were checked or changed. By 1899 at the latest, the house was no longer the post office for North Lancing (see No. 66), and by the 1920s it was given the name 'The Old Posting House', its previous name being 'Walnut Tree Cottage'. The repair to the front wall can be seen where the tree once protruded through it. Evidence now suggests that this building is the original Grants manor house.

## 62. *House and Smithy Shop (Forge)*

The buildings still exist and although the old forge was apparently almost rebuilt during the early part of this century the site is very old. They were in existence in 1770 and probably long before that. During the latter part of the 18th century they were owned by Richard Sharp and then the Carver family, although a member of the Sharp family was occupier throughout this period. John Sharp, occupier in 1825, was a blacksmith by trade and probably the son of Richard Sharp.

The map of 1803 shows a large area in front of the house and smithy, where horses and vehicles pulled in off the road and where much of the work was done. In 1866 the property was bought by the Lloyd family for £600 and was freehold.

Much of the external face of the old forge buildings still exists, as does part of the original walls, but has been transformed into a residence and is under different ownership from the smithy cottage.

Some of the early owners and occupiers are as follows:

| Date | Owner | Occupier |
|------|-------|----------|
| 1780–95 | Richard Sharp | Richard Sharp |
| 1796–98 | R. Carver | Richard Sharp |
| 1799–1820 | Mrs. Sarah Carver | Richard Sharp |
| 1821 | Mrs. Sarah Carver | Mrs. Sharp |
| 1822–25 | Mrs. Sarah Carver | John Sharp |
| 1826–66 | John Sharp | John Sharp |
| 1866–76 | Lloyd family | Thos. Butler |
| 1878 | Lloyd family | Mr. Crosskey |

## 63. *Parsonage Barn, Hovel and Yard*

This site is now occupied by flats, but on it once stood the 'Old Tythe Barn' or parsonage barn. The barn appears to have

Fig. 32. The Old Tithe Barn, *c.* 1920

been built sometime between 1803 and 1838 and originally a pond existed in the north-west corner of the site. Very little is known about the early history of the barn apart from the fact that its title indicates it was once used for storing the tithes due to the vicar.

During the early part of this century it was severely damaged by fire, probably when it had a thatched roof, because by the 1920s it had a corrugated iron roof. By 1923 the barn had become dilapidated, the pond derelict, and the space in the front of the barn used as a rubbish dump. The cottages in the site were empty and so was the blacksmith's forge (No. 62).

An artist had noticed the barn and purchased the land, and during the latter part of 1923 work was started on the transformation of the barn into an attractive residence. One of the cottages was turned into a studio in harmony with its surroundings, whilst the old smithy became known as 'The Forge'.

During the reconstruction of the barn the aim was to retain as much of its old material and character as possible. The main walls were in a fairly good state of preservation, but drastic alterations were necessary to complete the internal arrangements.

A bedroom, windows and chimney stacks were added. The outside area was transformed into a lovely garden and a tennis court. The name given to the residence was 'Ye Olde Tithe Barn'.

The house remained for 40 years before it was finally demolished on 3 May 1963. Modern buildings are now on its site.

## 64. Tenements

This site at present contains two buildings known in 1908 as '1-4 Joyces Cottages' when they were purchased from Mr. Stubbs by J. M. Carr-Lloyd for £600.

The single building adjacent to the road is at present known as 'Hawthorn Cottage' and is flint-built. The other building was also flint-built, and was originally divided into three tenements, but at present is one house. It is estimated that it was probably built in the 17th century, the east end of the building being early 17th-century.

The particulars of a sale of a portion of the Lancing Manor Estate on 20 July 1922 describe the property as 23, 22 and 21 Joyces Cottages, number 23 being the west end of the building. No. 23 was semi-detached and contained a living-room, scullery, three bedrooms and an outside earth-closet. It was let on a weekly tenancy of four shillings per week. No. 22, the middle tenement, contained a living-room, scullery, two bedrooms lean-to woodhouse, and earth closet, and was let on a weekly tenancy of three shillings and threepence per week. No. 21 was semi-detached and similar to No. 22. Hawthorn Cottage, then No. 20, was described as having two sitting-rooms, kitchen, scullery, four bedrooms lean-to outhouse and earth closet, let on a weekly tenancy of seven shillings a week.

## 65. Tenements

The 1770 and 1803 maps of Lancing do not appear to show these two tenements. Nos. 19 and 18, although they are believed to have been built before 1770. It is thought that No. 19 was probably late 17th- or early 18th-century, while No. 18 was probably mid-18th-century. In 1922 they are both described as detached, flint-built and tiled. No. 19 contained a sitting-room, kitchen, scullery, two bedrooms, lean-to woodhouse and earth closet, and was let on a quarterly tenancy. No. 18 contained a living-room, scullery, two bedrooms and outside earth closet. Both these properties still exist, and with the same house numbers as in 1922. No. 19 is named 'Twitten Cottage'.

## 66. Tenements

The 1770 map of Lancing shows a building in a similar position to that shown on the 1838 Tithe Map. Although the former map casts some doubt on the accuracy of the positioning of the buildings shown, this does fall in line with the belief that these cottages were built in the late 18th or perhaps early 19th century.

In 1803 the site and buildings were owned by Hampton, and in 1838 it is described as '2 tenements and garden owned and occupied by Samuel Hampton'. In 1864 Lloyd purchased the building and site from Hampton for £350 and it is described as 'Cottage and garden, copyhold when bought, now freehold'. In 1899 the Ordnance Survey map of Lancing shows this building as North Lancing Post Office. At some date after 1838 this building must have been altered internally, for in 1922 it is shown as three cottages, cement-rendered and slate-roofed, known as 'Post Office Cottages' (Nos. 17, 16 and 15).

No. 17 contained two bedrooms, a living-room, scullery and earth closet. No. 16 was the North Lancing Post Office and described as above, but let on a weekly tenancy of four shillings and sixpence per week. No. 15 contained two bedrooms, a sitting-room, kitchen, scullery, wash-house and earth closet, let on a weekly tenancy of four shillings per week.

An old photograph of this building in the early part of this century, exact date unknown, shows No. 15 to be the post office.

This building still exists with the same house numbers, but has a different frontal appearance from that shown on old photographs. The eastern chimney has also been removed.

## 67. Tenements

In 1803 a house is shown on this site owned by Allin, and in 1838 it is described as 'Two Tenements and Garden', owned by William Allin, a shopkeeper. It was demolished prior to 1869, for the Ordnance Survey map of that date shows the 'Baytree Cottages' on the site. This building is divided into three houses and still exists.

## 68. Tenements

The 1770 and 1803 maps of Lancing show a single building on this site, but in a different position and shape to the three buildings shown on the 1838 map. The central building of the three appears to be an outhouse or barn which could account for the earlier building shown. It would then appear that the houses on this site were built in the early 19th century. They were built in two pairs, the pair on the west of the site being at right-angles to 'Baytree Cottages' and The Street, and the other pair on the east of the site being adjacent to and facing The Street.

In 1922 they are described as cottages, flint-built and tiled, and forming two pairs. Each contained two bedrooms, a living-room and scullery, with outside earth closets. They were all let on a weekly tenancy, ranging from two shillings to three shillings and sixpence per week. The westernmost pair were numbered 14 and 13, and the other pair 12 and 11.

These buildings no longer exist and modern houses stand on their site.

## 69. Tenement

The earliest mention of this property so far identified is in 1777 when it was owned by Thomas Bushby, a yeoman, and William Carlton. The property was described in a deed as a tenement, barn, hovel and garden. By 1805 it was in the possession of George Bushby, eldest son of Thomas. In 1826 it was sold to James Martin Lloyd, and by 1838, although still owned by Lloyd, it was occupied by Thomas Bushby.

The cottage remained thatched until 1964 when it was burnt down. The site is now occupied by modern houses.

## 70. Wheelwright's Shop and Yard

The shop was built between 1805 and 1838 for James Martin Lloyd and became part of his Lancing Manor Estate. This building was demolished some years ago, and modern houses occupy the site at the end of The Street.

## 71. Lancing Manor House (see Chapter Two)

The Manor House, which was demolished in 1972, stood on the site of a very old cottage. The foundations of this cottage were plainly visible in the north-east corner of the Manor House after its demolition. It is almost certain that a member of the Lloyd family had the house built, probably in the early 18th century, although its exact age is not known. The earliest view of the Manor House to date is a sketch by Grimm in 1789 (Burrell Collection in the British Museum, see Fig. 4). However, we know that the farm and house belonged to James Lloyd in 1739, and the existence of the house is confirmed by a deed of the same year. At that time the house was known as the 'Whitehouse', the estate was called 'Whitehouse Farm' and a field adjoining the house at the east side was the 'Whitehouse' field, the name no doubt having derived from the colour of the house when new.

Originally the main highway ran past the front of the house, but under the terms of the Enclosure Act of 1803 in Lancing, J. M. Lloyd was allotted the area of ground then known as Links Furlong and he converted this into the manor grounds. A road was made from the bottom corner of the modern Mill Road down to the top of Grinstead Lane, joining up with the road to the *Sussex Pad,* thus diverting the traffic from Mr. Lloyd's house. The manor grounds were enclosed with railings and walls, with a lodge at the south side near the top of Grinstead Lane. By 1838 the outbuildings and houses known as the 'Manor Farm' were built in the north-east corner of the grounds, partly on the 'Garden of Shadwells' (formerly part of

Fig. 33. 'Shadwells' (now demolished), at the east end of The Street,
North Lancing

Fig. 34. Malt House Cottage, North Lancing

Shadwell's Farm). The houses have now been demolished, but a few old stables and other outbuildings remain.

Over the years another floor and a wing were added to the building. Other alterations were carried out to convert the building into the Manor House as many people remember it. The grounds were private, but were occasionally opened to the inhabitants of the village for such events as the annual hospital parades.

The house was demolished in 1972 after much publicity and local protest, the lodge and railings having vanished many years ago. Very little remains now to remind us of the house and grounds as they were over sixty years ago. The original house had been in the occupation of a member of the Lloyd family for nearly two hundred years and was certainly at least two hundred and thirty years old. A sports centre now stands on the site.

### *72 and 73. Malthouse Farm and Malthouse Cottage (see Chapter 2)*

There were several farms in the area known as Malthouse farm, and very little information exists concerning the cottage and farm shown on the map. The cottage still exists, but the farm was demolished some years ago. On the 1770 map of Lancing there are buildings shown in a similar position to the farm and cottage, and if they are the same buildings, it would mean that they date at least from the 18th century.

### *74. 'Sussex Pad' inn (not shown on plan)*

The building presently on the site was erected not long after the original building (which dated possibly from the 16th century) was gutted by fire in 1905. It was probably built as a stopping-place before one crossed the river to Shoreham by the ferry which existed before the wooden bridge was built in 1782. The inn was probably well used, as it stood on the junction of the old Arundel–Brighthelmstone (Brighton) highway and the narrow, winding road to Steyning via Coombes.

In his book, *The Story of Shoreham,* Henry Cheal states that the *Sussex Pad* was a favourite resort for smugglers because of its lonely position near the river, while its cellars and hiding places were very convenient for storing contraband until it could be safely conveyed inland. Although the exact meaning of the word 'Pad' is not known, it is thought to be connected with 'packhorse'.

The known occupiers of the original premises are:

| | |
|---|---|
| 1780–82 | Robert Hemery |
| 1783–93 | James Carver |
| 1794–95 | H. Partington |
| 1796–97 | Benjamin Scarvell |
| 1797–98 | John Mathews |
| 1799–1818 | James Lee |
| 1819–22 | Mr. Parkhurst |
| 1823–30 | Robert Allen |
| 1831 | ? Simmons |
| 1832 | S. Stubbs |
| 1838 | John May (Richard Tamplin, owner) |
| 1855 | James Peskitt |
| 1858 | Henry Scrivens |
| 1866 | Henry Elliott |
| 1872–79 | William Taylor |
| 1890–95 | Albert Cooper |
| 1896–1903 | William Hole |
| 1905 | Albert Shoulders (old building destroyed by fire) |

## 75. Lancing Mills (not shown on plan, but see map of Area I)

The first references to mills in Lancing are in the Domesday Book: 'Here is a mill of 8s. . . .', and the Nonae Returns for Lancing in 1341 in which we are informed: '. . . the tythe of a watermill destroyed by the sea at 4s. per annum . . .'.

Several windmills were known to be in general use in England during the 12th century, and these early windmills (and watermills) were usually owned by the lord of the manor. The mills had 'soke' rights attached to them which meant that everyone within the manor had to send their flour to the mill to be ground, and tolls were exacted by the lord of the manor. Later mills were owned and rented privately, and then the millers were entitled to the toll, which was usually one-sixteenth of the flour they ground.

The earliest mention of a windmill is in the old document referred to in Chapter Three concerning How Court and the marshlands. From the description of its location it appears to be in a similar position to that of a windmill on the 1770 map of Lancing.

A deed of 1641[10] which describes scattered pieces of land and mentions '1 rood near Lancing mill' and '. . . in Mill Furlong . . .'. Although the site of the mill is not indicated in the deed it is fairly safe to assume that the mill was also in the same position as the mill shown on the map of 1770. The site of the mill on the map was at the top of the path which now goes through the manor woods, at the point where it emerges on to the open grassland leading to the chalk-pit (see map of Area I). The small area of land on which the mill stood was known as the 'mill piece' and a field opposite (in the manor of How) was known as the 'Mill Field'. Very little is known about this early mill as there appears to be no existing drawings or descriptions of it. However, a reference to it is found in a counterpart of a lease[11] by Richard Biddulph to John Olliver, a miller, of a corn windmill called Lancing mill, in which one new pair of French stones and one pair of Peak stones were fixed. There was also mention of a new store-room built underneath the mill. Later maps of 1795 and 1820 show a mill in the same position. It is obvious that 'Mill furlong' derived its name from its position adjacent to the mill.

In the Tithe Map of Lancing a mill is shown on a site further west and close to the chalkpit. It shows, therefore that between 1820 and 1838 either the mill had been repositioned, or, what is more likely, that the mill was in a bad state of repair and was pulled down, a new one being built nearer the chalkpit. There is also the possibility that trees planted near the mill (now the manor woods) had grown to a height which prevented the mill from working efficiently. Whatever the reason a new site was chosen and a mill remained on this site until it was demolished in 1905.

From the few photographs that exist of the last mill it appears to be of the type known as a post-mill, with four sails and a tailpost. This type allowed the whole body of the mill to be revolved on a centre post by means of the tailpost (either pushed manually or winched), so that the sails could face the wind.

Fig. 35. Lancing Windmill, 1890

With the help of Land Tax Records of Lancing between 1780 and 1832 and other scattered references, the names of recorded Lancing millers have been extracted, and the following list compiled:

| Date | Miller |
|---|---|
| 1591 | Mrs. Andrews, widow |
| 1763–1787 inc. | John Olliver |
| 1788–1789 inc. | James Michaux |
| 1790–1791 inc. | John Heaver |
| 1792–1797 inc. | James Bridger |
| 1798–1812 inc. | John Stepney |
| 1812–1814 inc. | John Simons |
| 1815–1828 inc. | Thomas(?) Meetens |
| 1829–1838 inc. | James Lloyd (owner), lord of the manor (no other names mentioned) |

## Some Properties which appeared after 1838

### Lancing College

Lancing College buildings and chapel form a most conspicuous landmark overlooking the River Adur, in the north-eastern part of the parish. The College is built on part of the old Burvill's Farm, which is situated in the original Manor of How (Hoe Court).

In 1852 the property was purchased by Nathaniel Woodard, the founder of the College, the first stone being laid in March 1854 by the founder himself.

It is not my intention here to write any more than brief historical notes about the college as B. W. T. Handford's excellent book is a major work on the subject, containing a great deal of information relating to the College, and interested readers should refer to it.[12]

Kelly's *Directory* of 1940 for Worthing and its neighbourhood informs us that the Corporation of SS. Mary and Nicholas College is a governing body of a federation of Colleges which are united for the supply of public school education on Church of England principles. The Southern Foundation consists of four schools, namely Lancing, Hurstpierpoint, Ardingly and All Saints' School, Bloxham, near Banbury.

The most impressive building on the site is the chapel, which is particularly interesting, and an address given to the Friends or Lancing Chapel, by B. W. T. Handford on 10 October 1970 gives an account of the building of the chapel and the problems involved. With the kind permission of the author the major portion of the address is reproduced as follows:

It all started with the publication of Nathaniel Woodard's Plea for the Middle Classes, out of which grew his schools. But a great chapel formed no part of his original scheme. This is shown by the first building plan. In 1849 there was a prospect of acquiring a site for St. Nicholas College in Shoreham and 'old' Carpenter drew a plan for the College on this site. In this the Chapel is no larger in proportion to the other buildings than the ordinary college chapel at Oxford or Cambridge. By 1853, however, when work on the present site began, the founder's ideas had evolved and the new plan for the college shows a much larger chapel. But in fact 'old' Carpenter had not completed his design for the Chapel at the time of his death and his own latest drawing shows only a ground plan. The Perspective drawing must have been made by his partner Slater on the basis of Carpenter's work. Though large, this chapel is still on a fairly modest scale. I say 'fairly modest' because it is little loftier than the dining hall, but I will ask you to remember that the whole college is designed on a large scale, a fact which is disguised by the absence of ordinary houses around it. It is a favourite practice of mine when showing people round the College to take them on to the Chapel quad, where, of course they all gaze at the Chapel. I then direct their attention to the dining hall and say: 'The height of that hall is 90 feet from the ground to the apex of the roof —exactly the same height as Salisbury Cathedral—now look at the Chapel'. There seems no better way of appreciating the great scale of the Chapel, which was finally designed by 'young' Carpenter in 1868.

Why did the founder decide to build on so large a scale? He is explicit about his reasons. First he wanted to have a church large enough to hold all the boys and girls of the Southern Division of the schools for the occasional meetings which he hoped would do something to override those class distinctions which were catered for in his schools but which he desired to mitigate. Secondly he wished to make a visible challenge to the growing materialism of his time and thirdly he hoped that his chapel would contribute directly to the religious experience of the boys.

A year ago the Head Master asked me to talk to the new boys about the Chapel. I did this one Sunday evening after dark. When I had explained the purpose, the history and the architecture of the building, I turned all the lights out. Now when lit only by starlight, the Chapel seems very vast, very mysterious and very still. I said to them 'keep very still' and they did. To experience this vastness, this mystery and this stillness is to feel something of the presence of God, and I know from what they said to me afterwards that some at least felt this. Then I switched on the tapestry floodlights. Believe me, after the darkness and with the rest of the Chapel still dark, the colours of the tapestry are breath-taking—and I am not speaking in metaphors—I heard the intaking of breath all round. 'There', I said, 'is glory'. I have shown hundreds of people round the Chapel and the effect on them is nearly always the same. They enter the door, they stop, they look up. It arrests them, and they see a 'sursum corda' in stone. I am sure that Woodard meant his chapel to provide such experiences as these. 'The invisible things of God', he wrote, 'are seen and understood by things which show themselves in the world . . . and one of the original purposes of cathedrals was to bring God before the mind in all these forms'.

I have called it 'his' chapel. I have done so designedly. There is a tradition in the Woodard family that Nathaniel himself played some part in the designing of it; for though he was not a trained architect, he was sensitive to architecture and Lancing Chapel is in some ways rather different from the rest of Carpenter's work. A story is also told that Woodard had been ill at the time when the Chapel was being conceived, and when he was better and was able to get out of bed, he said that the height of the Chapel should be determined by the number of paces he could walk. He managed to walk 150 paces and the height of the Chapel is 150 feet.

When this design was published in *The Builder* in 1868, it caused something of a sensation. No church had been projected on this scale since St. Paul's Cathedral and I suppose no gothic church since King's College Chapel. And this was to be a school chapel. It was intended to be more than a school chapel, I know, but a school chapel it is nonetheless. It was expected to cost £300,000. Practical men thought that the scheme was impossible. I do not know how to translate the money of 1868 into our money, but I suppose that this sum was equivalent of between two and three million today. The school was only 20 years old and the total number of old boys was only 450. Where was the money to come from? I have read the account of the speeches made at the laying of the foundation stone in 1868. Much is said in praise of the schools and of Woodard's work, but none of the speeches except Woodard's mention the Chapel. The whole project was clearly an embarrassment to level-headed men. One such said to Nathaniel: 'But, Mr. Woodard, you trust entirely to luck to finish the work'. 'I do', replied Woodard, 'But I call it by another name'. He meant of course faith, though he did not use the word.

Some years ago I did some research to find out what was the common factor shared by the old boys I knew who had become distinguished and I came to the conclusion that the only common factor was that they were all 'mad on' something, by which I mean that they were so whole-hearted about some aim or interest that nothing could long divert them, no impediment could long delay them, that no other interest could distract them from their absorbing interest. Other and lesser men say that they are 'mad' about it. In this sense the Founder was 'mad about' the Chapel. Others might say that it was impossible, it was a Woodard 'folly', but Nathaniel's faith has been justified.

And so in 1868 the foundation-stone was laid and they began to dig for the foundations, with Billy Woodard, the Founder's son, in charge of the work. The story is well known, how instead of finding rock chalk just beneath the surface as on the site of the other buildings, they found nothing but clay and sand, how Carpenter told Woodard that it was impossible to build on this site and how Woodard refused to accept the impossibility. So, where each column and each buttress was to be, they started digging great holes—48 of them in all. I would ask you to think of the work those old Victorian navvies did. There was no machinery, the clay and the sand were loosened by pick, shovelled into buckets and hoisted to the surface. Boys would come and ask, 'have you reached rock yet?' 'No, not yet', was the daily reply. Lower and lower they went, revetting the sides with timber, until at last they reached rock at an average depth of 55 feet. In all they must have shifted and hoisted some 10,000 tons of material. What did they do with it? Billy Woodard was not one to waste anything. He set up a kiln and baked the clay into bricks— he reckoned he made about half a million of them—and the sand he kept for mixing the concrete, while the useless material forms the basis of the terraces East and North of the Chapel. Fifty years ago I was talking to William Brown, then clerk of the works, and he told me how 40 years before that, when working on the foundations of the tower, he had been able from the bottom of the shaft to see the stars at mid-day. I see some of you smiling. It was a genuine experience and a physicist will tell you how it is possible. I like to think of those navvies gazing up in wonder from the bottom of a 60 foot shaft at the mid-day stars.

Then Billy bought a barge, which he ran up and down between the beach and the 'barge ditch' at Cuckoo Corner bringing up shingle for concrete. He poured lime concrete into those shafts at the rate of 100 tons a week for two years. Brick arches linked these concrete columns and at last the foundations were in. 'I told you you could do it, if you tried', said Nathaniel to Carpenter.

And so in 1871 they started on the crypt. Nathaniel had been given the right to quarry stone by a land owner at Scaynes Hill. This Sussex sandstone is of uneven quality and had to be carefully selected. It was said that while it was soft to work it would harden with age, provided it was worked while the quarry damp was still in it and that it was laid in accordance with its natural position in the quarry. Many years ago now, when the ashlar of the interior had not long been laid, a mother and her son gave the carvings on the corbels in the Lady Chapel and the St. Nicolas Chapel as a thank-offering for his recovery from a desperate illness while he was at school. The sculptor, whose name was Blair—the same man who carved the bases and the capitals in the entrace to the dining hall—came to me and said: 'Is there any mason about who can tell me how to work this stone? I can't work it. It comes away like brown sugar'. So, I took him to old Dick Gale, the last of the College masons. 'How do you work this stone, Dick?' 'Yer bores 'oles', said Dick. Blair found that in this way he could work it. 'But', he grumbled, 'it's like brown sugar'. Yet when recently it was necessary to cut into the western columns to get a bonding for the new work, it took several days with an electric drill to cut into it, as Reg Smith will tell you.

This stone, then, was quarried at Scaynes Hill, loaded in huge blocks on to a wagon and pulled by horses the 20 miles or so to Lancing. Three generations of a family spent their lives quarrying the stone and it is said that not one of them ever came to Lancing to see what was done with it. I used to watch the masons working in the yard on the south side of the Chapel. Two men, using a frame-saw with a toothless blade, sat, one each side of one of these blocks, and pulled the saw backwards and forwards. To prevent the saw overheating, an old tin with a small hole punched in the bottom dripped a trickle of water into the cut.

And so in the next four years they built the crypt and faced the walls inside with chalk from the quarry near the pond. It was dedicated for use in 1875. In another five years they had built the whole wall of the Chapel up to the base of the triforium. The east window of the Lady Chapel was the gift of William Knight, the clerk of the works. It cost him £80, perhaps £500 in our money, a princely gift from a Victorian working man. Billy hoped that one day stained glass would be put in it in his memory.

I was brought up to admire the patient, slow way the Chapel was built. But was it so slow? In our present building programme we have done well. We have raised £170,000 and starting in 1958 we have reached the triforium by 1970. But they, starting in 1868, built all the rest of the Chapel to the same height, 10 bays to our one, by 1880. There is something heroic about the Victorian age, we are only the epigoni.

It must have been about this time that a ship carrying Portland stone was wrecked off Shoreham. Billy bought the wreck 'for a song', salvaged the stone and ferried it up to the College to await the time, still many years ahead, when the Chapel would be paved. This is the stone pavement on which you walk.

In 1882 the foundations of the tower, redesigned for the third time, were put in, going down 80 feet. It was to be 350 feet high, more than doubling the height of the Chapel. The story has often been told how Woodard planned to have a cruciform light in the tower—this first appears in the final design. In times of storm the choir was to go up the tower and sing a hymn for those at sea, while seamen passing down the Channel in the storm would see the light and know that they were being prayed for. Nathaniel in explanation tells how his mother (who had relatives in the Navy) used to gather her children round her in times of storm and tell them to pray for those at sea. This tower would have been intensely dramatic, but, alas! we have had to abandon the project and only with the imagination will ever hear the music of young voices floating down from the lighted tower rocking in the gale.

By this time Nathaniel was getting on in years and he began to fear that when he had gone, courage would fade and the Chapel would not be built up to its full height. So he told Billy to concentrate on the east end and as a result between 1882 and 1885 the apse was built up to its full height. When I was a boy at Lancing I used to be told that the Founder had laid the top stone himself and solemnly pronounced a curse on any who should move it. School rumours are not a very good historical source and I doubt if Woodard ever cursed anybody, but the story has perhaps the truth of a parable. One result of this operation has been uneven settlement. Where the apse joins the next bay there is a crack. It does not appear to be serious and does not appear to be widening, but it is there as a visible record of the Founder's fear.

And so the work went on, with clerestory and roof marching slowly towards the west. Whenever Billy ran short of money, he went to see Martin Gibbs and Martin would reach for his cheque book. No one knows how much he gave altogether. About 1900 the temporary west wall was put up and in the next 10 years the vaulting and flying buttresses marched westwards, helped by Bernard Tower's munificent gift of £10,000 (worth £50,000 or so in our money). Carpenter had died by this time, but Billy built the vault from his drawings. There was no architect to watch over the work, but experts marvel at the perfection of the vault with its subtle curves. And so after 43 years of building, the Chapel was dedicated for use in 1911. I remember Henry Bowlby telling me how on the morning of

Dedication Day he was aware of something unusual and realised that it was the first weekday since he had been at Lancing that he had not heard the sounding of the sawing of stone. Next day the sawing started again.

The war of 1914, of course, interrupted the work, but as soon as it was over, the war memorial cloister was built along the south side of the Chapel to the design of Temple Moore. It took several years to complete and every stone of it was laid by Dick Gale. But first the ground had to be dug down to crypt level. This was done mainly by the boys, with the Headmaster sometimes lending a hand. Much of the bank was sand-sawdust from the working, which in the course of 40 years had reached a depth of several feet.

Then attention was turned again to the main structure. Billy had died in 1917 and there was no one to push forward the work. However, Sir George Oatley, whose work at Bristol University had established his reputation as an exponent of gothic, was appointed architect. He told me that many years before as a young student he had been fascinated by Carpenter's design for Lancing and that when he was asked to make suggestions for its completion it was for him like a dream come true.

It was Cuthbert Blakiston who suggested building western transepts. Oatley's realisation of the idea is magnificent. But while we may admire the daring of Woodard's project, we may surely think that a plan which would literally double the size of Woodard's Chapel went too far. It would have provided a vast empty space—nothing more. But Providence intervened. The great depression came and this was no time for raising money for so costly a project.

During the thirties the furnishing of the Chapel took all the available funds. Yet Oatley's work was not entirely wasted. During the Second World War, for safety's sake, he took all Carpenter's drawings as well as his own out of Bristol to his country cottage. Sir George died and by the time the war was over nobody at Lancing knew what had happened to the drawings. At Bristol University a young architectural student named Rome chose the completion of Lancing Chapel in his degree thesis. His professor was so impressed with his work that he sent it to Mr. Dykes Bower, who equally impressed offered him the chance to work on the actual completion. By these means the drawings were recovered and became available to the architect, and another youthful dream came true.

But to return—during the thirties the furnishing of the bare chapel took all the funds. The canopies of the stalls, constructed to the designs of Gilbert Scott and presented to Eton by the Prince Consort, had been taken down to reveal murals which they concealed. They were given to Lancing and with the fine new carved stalls beneath them greatly enriched the interior.

It was Cuthbert Blakiston who suggested that the bare east walls of the apse should be covered with tapestries and recommended that Lady Chilston should be asked to design them. We owe him a great debt of gratitude for this. They were woven at the William Morris works at Merton Abbey and each took three master weavers 18 months to weave. Merton

Abbey was bombed during the war and there is now no loom large enough in the country to weave on this scale. At the time Lord Chilston was the ambassador in Moscow and all the drawings were sent from there. On one occasion an agitated telegram arrived from the works—'no angels from Moscow'.

Soon after the last war the Friends of Lancing Chapel was founded, its first object being to raise funds to repair the slates on the roof. For some reason, the Provost asked me to attend the preliminary meeting and I remember saying that it did not seem to me a very inspiring purpose to ask for funds to repair an unfinished building. Why should we not say that our main aim was to finish the building? I think perhaps that I was meant to say this. Perhaps this was the reason that I was asked to the meeting. For after 1951, when Mr. Dykes Bower had been appointed architect and Wilfred Derry had taken over the treasurership and begun to put the drive into fund raising, we were faced with a 'political' difficulty. The body responsible for the Chapel is the Chapter, and very naturally the Chapter was circumspect about our undertaking to finish the Chapel for which they were responsible. Just as the Founder's contemporaries doubted his ability to raise the money, so did the Chapter doubt our ability to do so. So, first we obtained leave to finish the east end with its balustrades and pinnacles. Then we got leave to put in piles for the foundations—100 of them. And so little by little the Chapter's confidence in us grew and I need not say that now their co-operation is whole-hearted.

We have much still to do, but let us rejoice to do it. Make no mistake about it, Lancing Chapel is a great work of art and the generous grants that we have received from the Dulverton Trust and the Pilgrim Trust bear witness to public recognition of this. A few years ago, when anything that could be labelled 'Victorian' was anathema to bright young things, some might sneer at 'imitation gothic'. Such sneers showed both ignorance and insensitiveness. Lancing Chapel is, of course, built in the purest gothic idiom, but you will look in vain for an exact model for those columns and those mouldings. Comparisons that have been made, for example with Beauvais or the Sainte Chapelle are very superficial. The total effect is entirely individual and entirely original and as Sir John Summerson has so justly written, it is not Victorian, it is timeless. It is indeed one of the great churches of western Europe and it is given to us to complete it. We do not know who contributed to York Minster or Amiens Cathedral, but we see their work and rejoice in it. We are building to last 1,000 years, and though our names too will be forgotten, yet through our gifts something of us will be incorporated in this historic building. I say 'historic', for I do not think that men will build like this any more. Lancing Chapel may well be the last great gothic building in the world.

## Railway Works

The present Churchill Industrial Estate now stands on the site of the old railway works. Before the works were built the site was a piece of land in South Lancing known as the Ham and the Hurst, which formed a major part of the land conveyed from the Carr-Lloyd estate to the London, Brighton and South Coast Railway (L.B. & S.C.R.) in February 1903, the total area of the land being approximately 137 acres and costing £21,683 2s. 6d.

By 1913 a works had been erected by the L.B. & S.C.R. for building and repairing wagon stock.[13] Later, however, the works were developed for the repair and construction of carriages. After the grouping of the railways in 1923 the workshops at Lancing were reorganised to carry out the renovation of all the bogie carriage stock for the new Southern Railway. They were also to carry out the construction of all new carriage underframes.

During the Second World War certain government work was carried out at the works and this necessitated some of the workshops being adapted for this purpose. The work included the construction of pontoons and 'Horsa' glider tail-units.

There were just under two thousand employees at the works, many of whom came from such places as Lewes, Brighton, Bognor, and Littlehampton. A special train served the employees who lived to the east of the works and ran daily between there and Brighton. The work on the carriages was carried out on a progressive repair system, the carriage moving from section to section at certain intervals, at a rate relative to output. At each stage the carriage received attention. By the early 1960s the average output per year was approximately two and a half thousand vehicles, based on a 44-hour week.

An open day was held each year for the public to view the works and the proceeds went to the Southern Railway's Orphanage and Old People's Homes. These open days were held for 14 successive years and the last one took place in August 1963.

It was a sad day for hundreds of people in the neighbourhood of Lancing when the sudden news came of Lancing Railway Works' impending closure. This news was given in September 1962, and by June 1965 when the works finally closed, a considerable number of the employees had found alternative employment. Later the site was developed as the present Churchill Industrial Estate and now provides local employment from the several firms on the site.

*Farmer's Hotel*

The original *Farmer's* hotel stood on a site just in front of the present buiding of the same name. The building was erected *c*. 1851 by William Dabbs, whose family had come to Lancing in 1790 from Oving and acquired Yew-tree Farm (see Chapter Two). Originally the present King's Road was called Farmer's Lane, and terminated in the middle of fields in the area known as Penhill. It was a private lane for the use of the farmers who farmed the land either side of it. It seems quite feasible that this lane, the position of the inn and the fact that William Dabbs himself was a farmer, helped to provide the original name of the building, the *Farmer's* inn.

Just before the Second World War a new building was erected on the site, but further back from the old buildings, thus allowing an area in front to be used as a car park. This new building retained the same name.

The following list shows the known occupiers up to 1912.

| Date | Occupier |
|------|----------|
| 1851–66 | William Dabbs and later Caroline Dabbs |
| 1867–73 | George Hoad |
| 1874 | William Huntley |
| 1875–79 | Charles Virgin |
| 1883 | Samuel Smith and John Lathem |
| 1890 | James Henry Peters |
| 1895–99 | Harvey Henry Trevett |
| 1903–05 | Harry Spencer |
| 1907–09 | Humphrey Spencer |
| 1912 | Percy John Lynn |

*Chapter Five*

## LANCING ROADS

THE NUMBERS shown in brackets in the following notes refer to the roads shown on the 'Plan of the roads in Lancing, *circa* 1800', thus enabling the reader to readily trace the routes.

*1. King's Highway or Common Highway from Arundel (via
    Sompting and North Lancing) to Brighthelmstone
    (Brighton) (Nos. 1-5 on plan)*

This ancient highway can be traced by commencing at the top of Upper Boundstone Lane, at the western boundary of the parish, and proceeding eastward along Manor Road (1) past the church to Mill Road, northward up Mill Road (2) past the Old Posting House and the Forge as far as the junction with The Street. At this point the old highway turned to the east and ran along The Street (3) to the north of the manor recreation ground before turning southward past the front of the old Manor House (now demolished) (4). This road met the present Old Shoreham Road (5) and then ran eastward along this road to the *Sussex Pad* inn to meet the river which had to be crossed, originally by a ford or ferry and later by means of the old toll bridge—now retained for pedestrians only. Until about 1803 this route formed the main highway from Arundel to Brighton and was used by coaches, horses and all other travellers. After this date the route was altered when a road was formed (6) which joined up the bottom of Mill Road with the top of the modern Grinstead Lane, thus diverting all through traffic from The Street and the lord of the manor's house. The road past the old manor house no longer exists and The Street is no longer a through road for traffic. This route was again altered during this century when the Upper Brighton

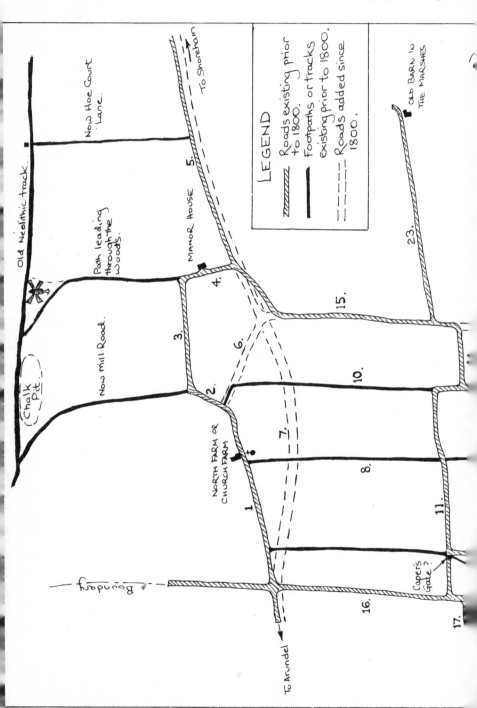

LEGEND

Roads existing prior to 1800.

Footpaths or tracks existing prior to 1800.

Roads added since 1800.

Old Neolithic track.

Now Hoe Court Lane.

To Shoreham

Path leading through the woods.

Manor House

Now Mill Road.

Chalk Pit

5.

4.

3.

2.

North Farm or Church Farm

6.

7.

1.

15.

10.

8.

11.

23.

Old Barn in the Marshes.

Caper's Gate?

16.

17.

Boundary

To Arundel

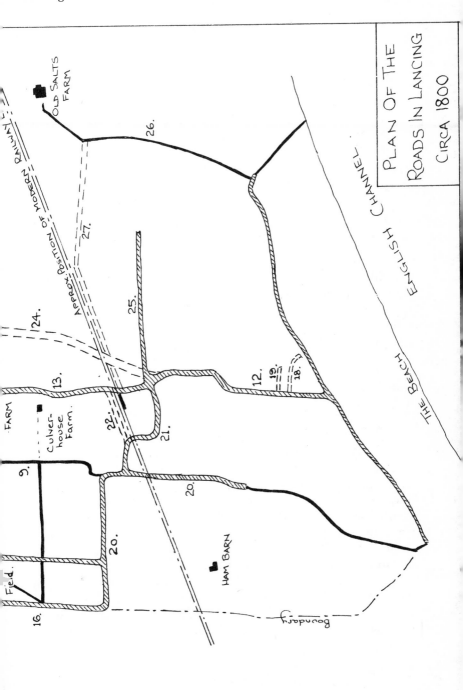

PLAN OF THE ROADS IN LANCING CIRCA 1800

Road by-pass was opened (7), thus causing the ancient route
to be used mainly by local traffic.

## 2. West Lane (Nos. 8 and 9 on plan)

This old lane was originally a footpath which led southward,
from the parish church at North Lancing, dividing the great
Lower West Laine and East Laine fields, to meet the present
Crabtree Lane. The footpath then continued southward past
the west side of what is now Monk's recreation ground and the
football ground, and then as a twitten out on to the present
Sompting Road (near the junction with Tower Road).

## 3. Church Path (now First Avenue) (No. 10 on plan)

This was originally a path leading to the church at North
Lancing from South Lancing via part of the common highway.
This was no doubt utilised as part of the main route by church-
goers from South Lancing. Eventually this path was widened
into a road and houses were built on either side. At one stage
the east side of the road, as far as Orchard Way, was still known
as Church Path, while the other side, and the remainder of
he road, was renamed First Avenue. Later the whole road was
given the same name.

## 4. Caper's Lane (now Crabtree Lane) (No. 11 on plan)

This old lane led from Boundstone Lane on the west to the
junction of the present First Avenue and North road, where
it terminated. The original name of Caper's Lane appears to
have derived from a field at the western end, adjoining Boundstone Lane, known as Caper's Field, together with Caper's
Gate (across the lane). From this gate a footpath led in a
south-westerly direction across the above-mentioned field. No
details are known of the name Caper.

At the eastern end of the lane was an orchard through which
a footpath led eastwards to Grinstead Lane. In recent years
the orchard has been cleared, the road widened, and Crabtree
Lane now runs right through to Grinstead Lane. The present

Fig. 36. The Downs from Crabtree Lane

name 'Crabtree' appears to have been given due to the number of crab-apple trees in the vicinity at the time.

## 5. Lower Lancing Street (Nos. 12–15 on plan)

This street was the main route from the sea in South Lancing. It can be traced by proceeding up South Street (12) from the sea-front and then on into North Road (13). Near Monk's Farm the street turned eastward into the present Grinstead Avenue (14), and then northward again into Grinstead Lane (15), up towards the old Manor House. It seems likely that most vehicular and horse traffic going to North Lancing would have used this route entirely, while travellers on foot would have used Church Path (10). In recent years Grinstead Lane (15) has been extended southward (24) across the railway line by means of a bridge to join up with South Street (12).

### 6. Boundstone Lane (No. 16 on plan)

This is, as the name implies, a boundary lane (on the west side of the parish) which once had the boundary stone or 'boundstone' located on the west side of the road near its present junction with the Upper Brighton Road. The position of the stone is shown on old Ordnance Survey maps of the area; it has been removed from the original position and is now in private possession.

Part of this lane forms part of the ancient road (17) to Cokeham Manor from Lancing.

### 7. East Street and Alma Street (Nos. 18 and 19)

These two roads were formed in the early part of the 19th century after Horseshoe field was sold to the Lancing Building Society (see Chapter Seven) and building development took place. During the middle part of the 19th century East Street (18) was known as Tribe Street.

### 8. Ham Lane (No. 20 on plan)

This very ancient lane was the lane leading down to the Ham in South Lancing. Its route is now represented by Sompting Road, running eastward from Boundstone Lane before it turns south to approach the railway (at the east end of the present Tower Road). Prior to the railway coming to Lancing this road continued southward down towards the Ham barn with a branch leading off to Lower Lancing Street (now South Street) via what is at present Elm Grove (21). However, the railway line severed this lane and all that remains to the south of the line is Elm Grove and a piece of the old, narrow Ham Lane, bordered by small trees which used to form part of the northern entrance into the Lancing Carriage Works (now Churchill Industrial Estate) from the south side of Lancing station. An added portion of road (22) running parallel with the railway now joins up with North Road.

### 9. Marsh Lane (now Mash Barn Lane) (No. 23 on plan)

The modern name Mash Barn Lane is a corruption of the name Marsh Lane and reflects the fact that the lane led to the barn on the old marshlands. This was originally a private road for the use of the farmers of the old marshes and surrounding areas, and probably dates from the 16th century when the marshland was reclaimed from the sea. Part of this lane still exists in its original form at the eastern end.

### 10. Salts Lane (now King's Road) (No. 25 on plan)

This road leads eastward from almost opposite the *Farmer's* public house.

Originally this was a private road for the use of farmers who had land in and around Penhill, and it terminated in the middle of that area. In the 19th century it was known as Salts Lane, and during this century as King's Road.

### 11. Old Salts Farm Road (No. 26 on plan)

This road, which leads to Old Salts Farm, is thought to be ancient and is possibly the top of the dry wall which was built to reclaim the fresh-brook marshes during the 16th century. In 1975 part of this road was made up and it now joins with the eastern end of Freshbrook Road (27), leading back to the crossing by the station. The north piece of the road still exists as a rough road leading to the farmhouse.

### 12. Other Roads

The plan of Lancing roads, *c.* 1800, shows all the roads which existed prior to 1800 as hatched. According to the Ordnance Survey map of Lancing for 1912 only six more roads had been added by 1912: Penhill, Cecil, Roberts, and Myrtle Roads, East Street, and Alma Street (not including the change in route of the common highway [6] in North Lancing between 1803 and 1805). The remainder of Lancing roads all appeared after 1912. Using detailed maps of Lancing as a guide to the dates of road formation, the following picture emerges:

| | |
|---|---|
| 1805-38 | One new road was formed |
| 1839-69 | One new road was formed |
| 1870-99 | One new road was formed |
| 1900-12 | Approximately three new roads were formed |
| 1913-31 | Approximately 24 new roads were formed |
| 1932-63 | Approximately 65 new roads were formed |

As most new roads are formed in conjunction with building development it is interesting to compare the foregoing figures with those of the increase in population shown at the end of Chapter Six.

Fig. 37. Market Garden Tokens of Nash Brothers, Lancing

About 20 of these tokens were found in a drawer of a piece of furniture which came from 'Nash Villa' in Kings Road some years ago. They were used as receipts for deposits on the empty containers used by 'Nash Brothers' for their market garden produce

## Chapter Six

# NOTES ON OLD FAMILIES OF LANCING AND POPULATION

THE EARLIEST reference to the inhabitants of Lancing occurs in the Domesday Book which informs that there are 17 villeins and 11 bordars in the 'Manor of Lancinges' and 14 villeins and eight bordars in the 'Manor of How'.

Later references to inhabitants occur in the late 13th and early 14th centuries in the Subsidy Lists for Lancing (a subsidy was a tax levied on people according to the value of their goods or land). In 1296[1] the tax was one eleventh, and in 1327[2] and 1332[3] it was one twentieth. The lists which are shown below only indicate the principal inhabitants, i.e., only those who owned goods or land.

### SUBSIDY LIST FOR LANCING, 1296

| Villat' de Lancyng | | | | £ | s. | d. |
|---|---|---|---|---|---|---|
| Ricro de Wohenehampton | .. | | .. | 1 | 2 | 2¼ |
| Thurstan de Brok | .. | .. | .. | | 6 | 0 |
| Robro de Bordevyle | .. | .. | .. | | 5 | 9¾ |
| Alic' atte Klyve .. | .. | .. | .. | | 2 | 0½ |
| Willmo le Weed .. | .. | .. | .. | | 4 | 10 |
| Hugon' de Westote | .. | .. | .. | | 11 | 1½ |
| Juliana de Woderove | .. | .. | .. | | 1 | 4½ |
| Johanne Aleyn .. | .. | .. | .. | | 2 | 8¾ |
| Willmo le Byrg .. | .. | .. | .. | | 2 | 0½ |
| Negello Flemeng | .. | .. | .. | | 14 | 0½ |
| Henr' Fraunceys | .. | .. | .. | | 1 | 11¾ |
| Regin' Kyng | .. | .. | .. | .. | | 1 | 6½ |
| Ricro de Ware .. | .. | .. | .. | | 2 | 2 |
| Waltero Swyft .. | .. | .. | .. | | 3 | 0¾ |
| Willmo Woderove | .. | .. | .. | | 1 | 8 |

*continued—*

*continued*–                                    £    s.    d.

| | | | | | |
|---|---|---|---|---|---|
| Matild' Woderove | .. | .. | .. | 4 | 0¾ |
| Johanne Lovetot | .. | .. | .. | 2 | 3¼ |
| Ricro Fluyr | .. | .. | .. | 1 | 11 |
| Rado Schot | .. | .. | .. | 2 | 1 |
| Alic' Relicta Hammer'.. | .. | .. | 1 | 1½ |
| Rado Andro | .. | .. | .. | 1 | 9¾ |
| Luca Cubbel.. | .. | .. | .. | 2 | 8 |
| Godefro Aleyn .. | .. | .. | .. | 15 | 10 |
| Waltero Nyuweman | .. | .. | .. | 3 | 8¾ |
| Rado Coppedene | .. | .. | .. | 15 | 1¼ |
| Julian' Buddyng.. | .. | .. | .. | 6 | 9¾ |

Sma. .. £7   0   0¼

## SUBSIDY LIST FOR LANCING, 1327

**Villat' de Launcyng**                    £    s.    d.

| | | | | | |
|---|---|---|---|---|---|
| Asselina de Brok | .. | .. | .. | 11 | 0½ |
| Johe Burdeville .. | .. | .. | .. | 3 | 6½ |
| Petr' A Westetoune | .. | .. | .. | 3 | 0 |
| Thom' le Monek | .. | .. | .. | 4 | 3¾ |
| Nicha fil' Mathi le Monek | .. | .. | 3 | 0¼ |
| Johe Swyft | .. | .. | .. | 4 | 3 |
| Rico de Gatewyk | .. | .. | .. | 1 | 8 |
| Rico Fluor | .. | .. | .. | 1 | 3 |
| Lucia que fuit uxor Robti Lucas | .. | 1 | 8 |
| Robto Seman | .. | .. | .. | 1 | 2 |
| Rico de Applesham | .. | .. | .. | 2 | 0½ |
| Nigello de Brok .. | .. | .. | .. | 3 | 9½ |
| Robto le Bakere.. | .. | .. | .. | 1 | 9¼ |
| Willo Lucas | .. | .. | .. | 4 | 2¼ |
| Johe de Clothale | .. | .. | .. | 1 | 2 |
| Willmo Coppedeux | .. | .. | .. | 1 | 3 |
| Walto Swyft | .. | .. | .. | 2 | 0 |
| Willo atte Welle .. | .. | .. | .. | 1 | 9 |
| Matho Swift | .. | .. | .. | 3 | 0 |
| Lucia de Merewe | .. | .. | .. | 1 | 2 |
| Robto Jauyn | .. | .. | .. | | 10 |

Sma. istius villat ..   £2   17   10½

### SUBSIDY LIST FOR LANCING, 1332

| Villat' de Launcyng | £ | s. | d. |
|---|---|---|---|
| Nigello de Brok .. | | 11 | 0 |
| Matho Bal | | 4 | 0 |
| Johe de Clothale | | 7 | 6 |
| Johe Bourdevyle | | 7 | 5½ |
| Cristina Prykefysh | | 2 | 6 |
| Rico de Coumbes | | 3 | 4½ |
| Henr' Woderose .. | | 6 | 8 |
| Petro a Westetoun | | 2 | 3 |
| Robto Baker | | 2 | 1 |
| Willo Coppeden .. | | 2 | 0 |
| Nigello Swyft | | 1 | 0 |
| Walto Swyft | | 2 | 0 |
| Symone Garskyn | | 4 | 0 |
| Willo Haneper | | 1 | 0 |
| Rico Fluyr | | | 8 |
| Robto Seman | | 2 | 1½ |
| Johe Swyft | | 3 | 8 |
| Martino Swyft | | 8 | 0 |
| Willo Lucas | | 4 | 8 |
| Rico Lucas | | 2 | 0 |
| Thom Monek | | 4 | 6 |
| Rado Swyft | | 3 | 0½ |
| Rado Alayn | | 1 | 6 |
| Ad Baker | | 1 | 0 |
| Sma. istius villata .. | £4 | 8 | 0 |

The number of inhabitants shown is 26 in 1296, 21 in 1327 and 24 in 1332.

Some very interesting information on surnames during the period of the Lancing Subsidy Lists is contained in C.M. Matthews' fascinating book *English Surnames*. He informs us that the period in which the mass of English surnames were firmly established was roughly between the reigns of William I and Richard II. This 'surname period', as it is called, can be divided roughly into two parts. The first stage is from the Conquest to approximately 1200, when the surnames of the upper classes and many of intermediate status were fixed. The later stage extended from 1200 to approximately 1360 when the surnames of the great mass of the common people followed, and the peak period of this stage was the reign of Edward I (1272–1307). Matthews classifies the surnames into sub-sections such as occupational names, nicknames, local names. etc.

The Subsidy Lists contain names which use Latin, French and English combined, usually in that order; in the 1327 list we find Robto le Bakere (Robert the baker) as a good example. Matthews' explanations for various surnames during this period throw some light on the early inhabitants of Lancing. Those which are particularly interesting are shown below, with explanatory notes based on Matthew's book.

*(a) Occupational Names*

The only examples which are immediately recognisable from the lists are Robto le Bakere (Robert the baker), 1327, who in 1332 takes the name of Robto Baker, Thom. le Monek (Thomas the monk?), 1327, who became Thom. Monek in 1332, and Robto Seman (Robert the seaman?) in 1327 and 1332. The name of Seman was a common one along this part of the south coast and the *Sussex Archaeological Collections* (Vol. XXI, p. 28) inform us that in April 1351 a William Seman died and a hundred acres of land in Lancing descended to Robert Seman, who consequently left the land to his brother, Richard Seman, for 20 years at a rent of 60 shillings a year. In 1524 the name still persists in the Lay Subsidy Rolls for Lancing as Rychard, Edward and John Seman. However, in 1641 when the Protestation Returns were made there were no inhabitants of Lancing with the surname of Seman, and no further record of this name has been found in connection with Lancing.

*(b) Nicknames*

One of the most interesting names in the 1296 list is that of Waltero Nyuweman (Walter Newman), the surname being spelt almost exactly as it is spoken. In the villages years ago a new-comer would be looked upon as a foreigner for many years, and this attitude would be expressed in the name Newman, which is the most common nickname. His name does not appear in the later lists, which suggests that he either died or moved on.

In early times only the upper classes rode on horseback and most of the community moved about on foot. They walked great distances, often running to deliver messages for their masters. Many of the best runners were recognised by being given such names as Speed, Lightfoot, Golightly and Swift. Lancing had its fair share of runners, for the name of Swift appears in all the lists as follows: Waltero Swift, 1296; Johe Swyft, 1327 and 1332; Matho Swyft, 1327; Nigello Swyft, Martino Swyft and Rado Swyft, 1332. This particular family name persisted in Lancing and its neighbourhood for over six hundred years.

Another interesting name from Matthews' book is Budd, a word specifying part of a tree or bush which can only be taken metaphorically. It was used as a common noun well before the Conquest and has survived for over a thousand years. Its original meaning, states Matthews, seems to have been connected with 'swelling', a small round thing that would grow and as such would make a good nickname for a plump child, for instance. The meaning of swelling shows a close relationship between 'budding' and the unromantic 'pudding'. In Lancing the name is represented by Julian Buddyng in 1296.

One other name which could be used as a nickname or in fun and mockery is King. This could have been given to the poorest person in the village, or it might have been given to a person who often played the part of a king in a miracle play. This name is represented in Lancing in 1296 by Regin' Kyng.

### (c) Foreign Names

It was said that the Low Countries always seemed to produce enough industrious people to send to England when the king needed to start a new industry or new area of colonisation. There were many Flemings, and although they were not liked and many were murdered during the Peasants' Revolt, a great number survived and the name spread. In Lancing we find Negello Flemeng (Nigel Fleming) in 1296, for instance.

The name Francis was indicative of race in the 'surname period' and Francais and Francis eventually became 'French'. As the French developed fixed surnames about the same time as we did in England it is supposed that people in England given the name of French or Francais must have settled here earlier. In Lancing in 1296, Henr' Fraunceys is mentioned—his nationality was probably easily identified. The same reasoning applies to Scotts or Scot, and a Rado Schot is listed in Lancing in 1296.

Before the Conquest the English made their own wine as best they could with sour grapes, but later a good business built up between Bordeaux and the principal English ports. As the name 'Bordeaux' does not seem to appear in the lists it is probable that the merchants were simply called Gascons, Gascoigne, Gaskain, or Gaskin. Thus we note Symone Garskyn in Lancing in 1332.

Matthews also states that in the process of anglicisation the French ending 'ville', which was unfamiliar to the English, was often turned into 'field', simply because it was more familiar and sounded similar. Thus Semerville becomes Summersfield; Blonville, Bloomsfield and Greenville, Greensfield or Grenfell. Using this knowledge it is obvious that in Lancing the name Bordeville (Robro de Bordevyle, 1296; Johe Burdeville, 1327; Joho Bourdevyle, 1332) could easily become Broadfield, Birdvilles, or Birdfield (see Chapter Two).

### (d) Bibilical Names

There are a number of names taken from the Bible and only two appear in the Lancing lists.

Luke, from the New Testament, usually occurs in the scholarly Greek form of Lucas. This is no exception in Lancing, for we find 'Lucia que fuit uxor Robti Lucas' in 1327; Willo Lucas in 1327 and 1332; amd Rico Lucas in 1332;

Andrew was a favourite name in England and Scotland, and in Scotland the form of Anderson was used, whilst in England, chiefly amongst the upper classes, Andrews was used. Rado Andro appears in Lancing in 1296.

## (e) Names from Nature

One of the early names in Lancing, or indeed any place, whose origin is difficult to pinpoint is Brok. In Lancing Nigello de Brok appears in 1332; Asselina de Brok, 1327; Thurstan de Brok, 1296; Christiana de Brok, 1290, and Matilda de Brok, 1315.

However, Matthews states that in this class of name the commonest are those that refer to the most important features of village life. As every village must have its water supply the names Brooks and Wells are plentiful. In Lancing, for instance, there is mention of 'Willo atte Welle'—William at the well (since there was originally probably only one main well this William would need no further identification). It is possible that the name Brok might refer to Brook, but it is also possible that it refers to the Brock (badger). Some of the characteristics which Matthews suggests might cause a man to be called Brock are short legs, shaggy hair and a strong smell! Brok appears to be a very ancient name in Lancing because, as mentioned in Chapter Three Nigel de Brok and John de Camoys claimed to have wrecks of the sea for their land and maintained '. . . that they and their ancestors have used the aforesaid liberties *before* the conquest of England and beyond the memory of man'.

Another name which, on the suface of it, seems to give no clue to its origin is Woderove (Julian de Woderove, 1296; Willmo Woderove, 1296; Matild' Woderove, 1296, and Henr' Woderose (?), 1332. However Matthews explains that Woodruff was probably given as a nickname to the rushman who provided the rushes for the floor of the great halls. The woodruff is a small plant that grows in woods, and when dried retains its pleasant fragrance; it was used for strewing in bed chambers or stuffing mattresses. When one considers that the scribes who wrote the names for the early lists of inhabitants must have spelt the name to correspond with the way that it sounded to them, it is easy to see that Woderove and Woodruff are so similar.

The names Flower and Blossom would make joking nicknames for beautiful, fair-haired youths. Originally these names were for girls, but from the 12th and early 13th centuries they appeared as surnames for men, obviously taken from their mothers' Christian names. In Lancing one such name was that of Rico Fluyr (Flower) spelt as Fluyr in 1296 and 1332 and Fluor in 1327.

## (f) Christian Names used as Surnames

There appears to be only one name in the early Lancing lists which falls into this category, namely that of Aleyn (Alan—a Breton name). Count Alan of Brittany (Alan the Red) brought a useful contingent of men to England, and this Christian name was prominent among William the Conqueror's noblemen. The Lancing people with this name were Godefro Aleyn, and Johanne Aleyn in 1296, and Rado Alayn in 1332.

## (g) Surnames from Local Words or Features

An old word *cleeve* or *clive* means a cliff and in 1296 'Alice' atte Klyve', possibly 'Alice at the Cliff' is listed at Lancing. There was known to be a low-lying cliff near the sea between Lancing and Worthing, portions of which are still visible after severe storms when the shingle is pushed back. Perhaps this is the cliff referred to in this person's name, where she, or a member of her family, originally lived.

Another example of a name containing a local feature is 'Petr' a Westetoune' in 1327 and 1332, probably meaning 'Peter at the west-of-town'.

The adjoining parishes of Coombes and Applesham are responsible for the origin of some names in the lists. In 1327 we find Rico de Applesham (Richard of Applesham) and in 1332 Rico de Coumbes (Richard of Coombes); since both parishes were under common ownership at that time, these two names probably denote the same person.

## (h) Miscellaneous Names

There were several pre-Conquest names which ceased to be first names after about 1200 and became surnames. One such name is Cuth-beald, meaning famous and bold, which later became Cobbold. A single example of a name similar to this is that of Luca Cubbel in 1296, which quite probably comes from the same root. Another interesting name, Willmo le Byrg, appears in 1296. *Burg* meant fortress and perhaps this name belonged to a particularly strong man, i.e., William the strong.

There are several names in the Lancing lists still unaccounted for and it will require a great deal of research to determine their origins. However, for the present they must remain a mystery to us.

The next recorded lists of Lancing inhabitants are the Lay Subsidy Rolls[4] of 1524 and 1525, where 47 persons are listed. In 1641 male members of the community over the age of 18 were required to sign a protestation[5] and 71 inhabitants complied. Only one person, Thomas Swifte, who was described as a 'poore fellow' did not take the protestation, despite being warned. From these two lists we find that the surnames of nearly two hundred years before have all disappeared with three exceptions. Aleyn survives as John Alen in 1524, but does not appear in the 1641 list. Swyft appears in all the lists with no less than seven male members mentioned in 1641, and Seman (mentioned in 1327 and 1332) appears in 1524, represented by Richard, Edward and John, but has no surviving male member of the family in 1641. Richard Seman died *c.* 1544, and Edward in 1540,[6] ~~but there is no further mention of John.~~ *in 1553 —Grant*

Other surnames, which first appear in the 1524 list and persist for the next two to three hundred years in Lancing are Blackman, Washer, Stamp, and Skinner. However by far the most persistent name is Swift (Swyft), which first appeared in the 1296 list and still has a representative (Mrs. Swift) named in the 1838 Tithe Award. This surname was common in the surrounding area of Lancing and there must have been (and may still be) many branches of the family.

As mentioned previously the Domesday Book shows that Lancing and How totalled 50 villeins and bordars or 50 households. J. R. Armstrong in his book *A History of Sussex* indicates that 50 households would represent about 250 people. The Sussex Subsidy Lists of 1296, 1327 and 1332 only show how many people owned moveable goods, and there were between 21 and 26 listed. In 1378 there were 117 adults, including 42 wives recorded in Lancing[7] and 45 households were shown in 1566.[8] Seventy-one male inhabitants over the age of 18 signed the Protestation in 1641, although this does not indicate the total population of Lancing at that stage. At the time of Bishop Bower's Visitation in 1724[9] there were said to be about 30 families.

In 1801 there were 451 inhabitants recorded and there was then a steady increase in population until 1881, when there were 1,381 inhabitants. For about twenty years the population remained roughly the same, and between 1901 and 1911 there was an increase in population of over 60 per cent., to just over two thousand. This falls in line with the increase in building development, and Chapter Five shows that three new roads were formed during this period compared with a total of three for the previous 94 years. Between 1911 and 1931 the population rose to approximately five thouand, again falling in line with the further 24 roads which were constructed in the same period. During the next 20 years the highest rate of increase in population was reached when in 1951 nearly twelve thousand people were recorded in the official census for Lancing. The number of new roads formed for a somewhat similar period (1932-63) was sixty-five. The rate of population increase then shows a slight drop when in 1969 an estimated fourteen and a half thousand inhabitants were shown.

In order to put the above figure into perspective the following small table is offered (it is not strictly mathematically correct because population increases vary from year to year, but it is accurate enough for the purpose intended).

| Between the Years | The approximate average increase in population was |
|---|---|
| 1801–1881 | 12 people per year |
| 1881–1901 | No increase—only slight fluctuations |
| 1901–11 | 78 people per year |
| 1911–21 | 113 people per year |
| 1921–31 | 185 people per year |
| 1931–51 | 345 people per year |
| 1951–69 | 144 people per year |

The rate of population increase must eventually drop as the available space for building development decreases.

A sample portion of land in Lancing in 1838 was analysed in terms of the area taken up by buildings and gardens and the area used for agriculture and other purposes. This was compared with the results of a similar analysis carried out for the same sample in the 1970s. The results were as follows:

| Date | Land taken up by buildings and gardens | Land taken up with agriculture and for other purposes |
|---|---|---|
| 1838 | approx 8 per cent. | approx 92 per cent. |
| 1970s | approx. 91 per cent. | approx 9 per cent. |

This shows an almost complete reversal in the intervening 140 years. In some respects these figures make generous allowances for the 1970s because the sample in question contained Monks Farm recreation ground, which due to its very nature could not be developed. However, to offset this biased sample is the area of the parish which is still used for agricultural purposes, i.e., New Monks Farm and New Salts Farm, and of course the area used for the aerodrome.

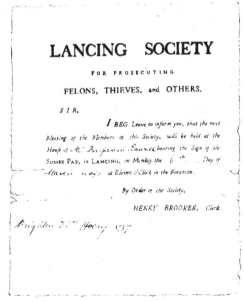

Fig. 38. Poster of the Lancing Society, 1797.

*Chapter Seven*

## SOME LANCING SOCIETIES AND CLUBS

### (1) Lancing Society for Prosecuting Felons, Thieves and Others

THE DATE of the formation of this society is not known. but it was in existence by 1789 and conducted its meetings at the *Sussex Pad* inn at Lancing. It appears that the society was Lancing's answer to combating crime in the years before the organisation of the police system by Sir Robert Peel. Rewards were offered by the society for information which it was hoped would lead to offenders of various crimes being caught and convicted.

The *Sussex Weekly Advertiser* contained notices of the society regarding crimes carried out in the area and stated the amount of the reward offered. One notice in particular in 1789[1] stated that a hen-house of the Rev. Hoper of Steyning was broken into and a considerable amount of poultry stolen. A reward of six guineas was offered to be paid on conviction of the offenders; three guineas were to be paid by the Rev. Hoper and the other three by the treasurer of the society, Mr. Brooker, to whom any information regarding the crime was to be 'immediately communicated'.

Advance notices of the meetings of the society were also placed in the same newspaper and posters were printed[2] which were no doubt placed in the *Sussex Pad* and other prominent buildings in Lancing.

### (2) Lancing Building Society

Being by the sea Lancing gradually became a fashionable place to live, especially South Lancing. In common with other local seaside resorts during the early part of the 19th century a considerable amount of building took place. A building society was formed in Lancing by a group of people who combined in order to help each other build and own their houses, and the members of the society each contributed money in order to buy land. As the houses were built they were allocated to the members, either by ballot or auction. It appears that the society also sold houses to non-members. These building societies began in the latter part of the 18th century and when the houses had been built the societies were wound up and became known as 'terminating societies'. The Lancing society seems to fall into this category.

A bundle of correspondence and a few deeds[3] held by the Sussex Archaeological Society in Lewes shows that the building society was in existence by 1809, when the Horseshoe field became part of its property. A great deal (if not all) of the building which subsequently took place on this site was controlled by the society. One of the houses in the Terrace, which faces the sea, named the 'Jubilee House' was mentioned in the society's accounts in the 1820s as having been sold to a Mr. Geast for £625. Accounts for the year 1822 show certain members' names and the number of shares held, as can be seen from the following extract:

|  | £ | s. | d. |
|---|---|---|---|
| 2 years rent of house occupied by Mr. Hodges received by the trustees, 1822 .. .. .. .. .. .. | 27 | 0 | 0 |
| the like of Mr. Geast for rest of garden .. .. .. .. | 1 | 5 | 0 |
| Purchase money of Hodges Houses by Mr. Whitpaine .. | 206 | 0 | 0 |
| Total .. .. | £234 | 5 | 0 |
| Minus solicitor's fees etc. .. .. .. .. .. .. | £210 | 12 | 7 |
| To be divided into 34 shares, each share .. .. .. | £6 | 4 | 0 |

|  |  |  | £ | s. | d. |
|---|---|---|---|---|---|
| Mr. Monkhouse | 4 shares | .. .. .. .. | 24 | 16 | 0 |
| Mr. Steel | 3 shares | .. .. .. .. | 18 | 12 | 0 |
| Martin Stubbs | 2 shares | .. .. .. .. | 12 | 8 | 0 |
| Thos. Clayton | 2 shares | .. .. .. .. | 12 | 8 | 0 |
| Mr. Polehill | 1 share | .. .. .. .. | 6 | 4 | 0 |
| Mr. Gibson | 1 share | .. .. .. .. | 6 | 4 | 0 |
| 21 others at £6 4s. 0d. each | .. | .. .. .. .. | 130 | 4 | 0 |
|  |  |  | £210 | 16 | 0 |

In the previous year (1821), 34 members each received £25, totalling £850.

The Overseers' Records of Lancing show instances of 'club-houses' being built between 1809 and 1820 which obviously belonged to the society. On 17 June 1815 a declaration of trust was made between James Stubbs, Richard Monkhouse and Martin Stubbs[4] and the following members of the society:

Thomas Clayton, merchant, New Shoreham
William Steel, victualler, Lancing
Nathaniel Polehill, merchant, West Tarring
Thomas Allin, shopkeeper, Lancing
George Tate, timber merchant, New Shoreham
Thomas Bushby, gardener, Lancing
Thomas Hill, Yeoman, Heene
John Gates, butcher, Steyning
Thomas Midmore, victualler, Worthing
Thomas Turner, victualler, Sompting
George Carr, victualler, New Shoreham
Christopher Knight, cooper, Southwick
John Lamport, victualler, Broadwater
Henry Patrick, brewer, Worthing
Thomas Allever, glazier, New Shoreham
James Cooper, shopkeeper, Lancing
George Bushby, yeoman, Lancing
Thomas Henty, gentleman, Goring
Charles Marshall, gentleman, Steyning
Stephen Lowdell, ironmonger, Lewes
John Hampton, cordwainer, Lancing
Benjamin Coomber, gardener, Lewes

There are no further mentions of the society after 1822 in the previously mentioned bundle of correspondence from the Sussex Archaeological Society, and as yet no other information has appeared. It is quite probable, therefore, that the society wound up shortly after this date.

### (3) Lancing Football Clubs

The earliest mention of football being played in Lancing is in the late 1850s, when Lancing College Football Club played on the College property;[5] later in 1883 the College formed an Old Boys' Football Club known as Lancing O.B.

An old photograph of a Lancing Football Club of about 1897 was discovered a few years ago under the stand of the present Lancing Football Club's ground in Culver Road. This is the earliest known club connected with the village itself. However, very little information is known about this club's history and the estimated date of its formation has been put at the 1880s. The matches were played on the vicarage ground which was situated to the south of North Lancing church; the site of the ground is now covered by the Upper Brighton Road. There appears to be no mention of the club after the First World War, and it seems likely that it was disbanded.

In about 1920 Lancing United Football Club was formed. An old member of the club informed me that they originally wore red shirts, which were later changed to black with a yellow 'V' on the front. Later still their shirts were again changed to red and black squares which apparently remained until the club disbanded in the late 1930s. The club originally joined the Brighton and District League and later, when the Worthing and District League was formed, they transferred to that league. In 1927-8 the club won the Benevolent Cup, and they were the first team to win the Croshaw Cup. Their matches were played on the Croshaw recreation ground.

The Lancing Football Club[6] that exists today began in 1938 when a number of young men used to kick a ball around on Monk's recreation ground. After a while a friendly match was played which led eventually to a whole season of 'friendlies'. In order to obtain their equipment the youths sold twopenny sweep tickets—commonly known as 'swindles'—and paid a subscription of threepence per week. By 1939 the team was equipped and Brighton and Hove Albion were interested in a number of the players. However, the war intervened, the club gave way and Brighton gained the services of such Lancing players as Stan Hickman, Reg Bowles, Dudley Davies, and Ernie France.

After the War most of the original team reassembled, and in August 1946 Roy Downing took over as trainer. It was soon evident Lancing had a very good team and their main objective was to gain County League status as soon as possible. The 1946-7 season in the Brighton and District League was tremendous, as the team was determined to win everything that it

entered for in the Brighton League Championship, Sussex
Intermediate Cup, and Brighton College Cup—and it did!
County League status for the next season seemed inevitable,
but they were turned down. If the previous season had been
very good then the 1947-8 season was unforgettable. The
club decided to show what they could do against County
League opposition and so they entered for the F.A. Amateur
Cup. What a run they had! In the prelimiary round Lancing
were at home to Shoreham, and in front of a large crowd at
the Croshaw ground they won by three goals to one. The first
qualifying round produced another home match, this time
against Haywards Heath. It was a thrilling game and ended with
two goals to one in favour of Lancing. The second qualifying
round meant an away match against Southwick, who were the
County League leaders at the time. It was a hard game for
Lancing and many people thought it would be impossible for
them to win, but somehow Lancing held out for the last few
minutes to win the tie by one goal to nil.

Two weeks later East Grinstead were defeated by five goals
to two. The next opponents were Tooting and Mitcham at
Lancing, and after a great game Lancing finally ended their
magnificent cup run by losing by two goals to one. The splendid
display by the Tooting and Mitcham goalkeeper was com-
memorated in a Sunday newspaper cartoon the next day when
it was suggested that he should not consider going anywhere
near Lancing for his holiday for the next few years!

By the end of the season Lancing had again won the Brighton
League Championship and the Brighton College Cup. They were
not allowed to enter the Sussex Intermediate Cup on account
of the number of senior sides they had played. Again County
League status seemed inevitable for the following season, and
this time it happened. In the 1948-9 season Lancing gained
admission to the Sussex County League to the immense delight
of the players, officials and their followers. Over the years
several Lancing players have been selected for Sussex, and
some of the first were Ernie France, Reg Bowles, and Dudley
Davies.

Eventually a Division Two was added to the County League
and at the end of the 1956-7 season Lancing were unfortunately

relegated to this lower division, but made history yet again by becoming the first club to return to Division One at the first attempt. A great deal of the credit for this must be given to Ken Shearwood (ex Pegasus player), the Lancing coach, who gave us all the confidence and will to succeed. I use the term 'us' in this instance as I had the good fortune to be the Lancing goalkeeper during this period of the club's history.

As time goes by many people forget or do not even know about those early officials and players whose dedication got Lancing Football Club into the Sussex County League. As a young boy I supported Lancing in those early days with hundreds of other Lancing fans, and we were certainly proud of them. When, in later years, I finally played for the club I couldn't have been happier.

At the time of writing this book Lancing is again in Division Two, but as in the past they have recovered from a bad 'patch' and I am sure that one day Lancing Football Club will be making the headlines once more.

# GLOSSARY OF TERMS USED

**Pot-boilers:** These were the flints used by early man to heat his water. The primitive clay vessels could not withstand the direct heat of fire and so flints were heated and dropped into the clay vessel holding the water. The sudden change of temperature caused these flints to crack and they are easily identified by their grey, cracked appearance.

**'Vouched for';** A term used in the Domesday Book which could be read as 'assessed at'.

**Geld:** Often known as 'Dane-geld' which was money paid to keep away the marauding Danes.

**Demesne:** Demesne lands were those areas of land directly belonging to the manor.

**Villeins:** Otherwise known as *Villani* or villagers. In the community these people had holdings of land in the common fields and owed services and payments of various kinds to the lord of the manor.

**Bordars:** Similar to the above *Villeins* but with smaller holdings of land.

**Hide:** A measurement of land area which appears to have varied from place to place. Originally equal to 100 Saxon acres (124.62 statute acres) of land which could be utilised. A hide in the Lancing area appears to have been about 120 statute acres.

**Salterns:** Salt-coats—places where salt was extracted from the sea at low tide. Shallow pans were dug to catch the salt water and at low tide the water was evaporated by the sun and the salt remained to be collected.

**'Died seized of':** When a person was described as having 'died seized of' certain property it meant that he died whilst in the possession of that property.

**Knight's fees:** A means of holding land from the lord of the manor in return for military services due to the lord when required. The knight may have been required to have a number of armed men ready as necessary or to perform military service for a given number of days per year.

**Died without issue:** A person who has died without any children from his marriage.

172

# APPENDIX I

## A CALENDAR OF SOME INTERESTING DATES AND EVENTS CONCERNING LANCING

| | |
|---|---|
| 1316 | William Paynell granted the ferry and 32 acres of land in Lancing to the priory and canon of Herryngham. |
| 1350 | Land granted to the priory of Mottenden in Kent by Michael de Poynings and others. |
| 1359 | Commission set up to repair sea walls at Pende. |
| 1371 | Simon of Lancing made a 'searcher' at Pende. |
| 1411 | Survey of Sussex manors shows Ralph Radmyld holding 'Lansyng Manor'. |
| 1499 | Manor of Lancing passed to John Goring of Burton. |
| 1591 | An action brought by Thomas Sherley against Sir Henry Goring for 'inning' part of the salt marshes. |
| 1591 | Earliest mention of the manor of St. Johns in Lancing. |
| 1608 | Survey carried out of the manor of How (Hoe-court). |
| 1643 | Soldiers at Lancing under Captain Charlton. |
| 1684 | Sir Henry Goring had 600 acres of marshland embanked or reclaimed to form 'The Salts' (now Old Salt's Farm) at a cost of £600. |
| 1725 | The manor of Lancing descended to a member of the Biddulph family from the Gorings. |
| 1736/7 | James Lloyd acquired the lease of the How Court Manor. |
| 1758 | James Lloyd purchased the manor of Howcourt. |
| 1760 | New harbour mouth made in the Adur at Kingston, Shoreham. |
| 1782/4 | Toll bridge built across the Adur near the *Sussex Pad*. |
| 1803/5 | Division and Enclosure Act implemented in Lancing. |
| 1807 | The *Three Horseshoes* inn built. |
| 1817 | The vicarage was rebuilt. |
| 1827 | The manor of Lancing purchased by J. M. Lloyd. |
| 1828 | (Good Friday). Discovery of Romano-Celtic temple on the Downs by J. Medhurst. |
| 1833 | The remains of the temple taken by J. Medhurst to his house in North Lancing. |
| 1838 | Tithe Map and Award drawn up for Lancing. |
| 1844 | J. M. Lloyd died and left the manor to his daughter. |
| 1845 | Railway opened through Lancing. |
| 1846 | Daughter of J. M. Lloyd died and left the manor to her stepmother, Lady Elizabeth Lloyd. |

1854    First stone of Lancing College laid by the founder, Nathaniel Woodard.

1855    Colonel Carr took the surname Carr-Lloyd by Royal Licence.

1858    Lady Elizabeth Lloyd died and left the manor of Lancing to Colonel Carr-Lloyd.

1868    Court case between the lords of the manors of Lancing and Shoreham regarding ownerhip of land to the south of the River Adur in Shoreham.

1877    (12 June). Colonel Carr-Lloyd, lord of the manor, committed suicide.

1905    *Sussex Pad* inn burnt down.

1905    The windmill next to the chalk-pit was pulled down.

1905    The Methodist church in South Lancing was built.

1907    Old and New Salt's Farm sold to Shorehan and Lancing Land Co. by J. M. Carr-Lloyd.

1920    Manor House and garden sold to Lancing College after the death of J. M. Carr-Lloyd.

1928    Saxon cemetery unearthed at Hoe-court House.

1929    L. A. Biddle and B. W. T. Handford rediscovered the Romano-Celtic temple site on the Downs.

1935    Manor House and grounds sold to Worthing Rural District Council.

1937    (December). South House demolished in South Lancing.

1939    Work started on Luxor cinema.

1951    (Friday, 30 March). Opening of the Post Office in South Lancing.

1960    Laurel and Myrtle Lodges demolished.

1963    Tithe barn demolished in North Lancing.

1964    Old thatched cottage at the end of 'The Street' completely destroyed by a fire.

1965    Lancing Carriage Works closed.

1971    An archaeological dig was carried out on the old marshlands, part of New Monks Farm.

1972    Lancing Manor House demolished.

# APPENDIX II

## LIST OF VICARS OF LANCING

The list of vicars has been compiled from the following sources:
(1) *S.N.Q.*, Vol. IV, p. 235.
(2) *S.R.S.*, Vol. XLIII (*Sussex Wills*, Vol. III).
(3) P. T. Jones, B.A., *The Story of Lancing Parish Church*, sixth edition, 1969, revised by the Rev. K. T. Toole-Mackson, B.D., F.Ph.S., F.R.S A.
(4) *V.C.H.*, 'The Rape of Bramber' (unpublished at the time of writing this book).
(5) Cartwright.

Some of the earlier vicars were often described as ministers, curates, preachers or officials.

| Date | Vicar | Patron |
|------|-------|--------|
| 1284 | Engeraud de Brok | (not known) |
| 1288 | William de Chrystechyrche | (not known) |
| 1334 | Robert de Chelwode | (not known) |
| 1350 | John atte Cate | Priory of Mottenden |
| 1364 | John de Cotes | ditto |
| 1374 | John de Stopeham | ditto |
| 1414 | Gilbert Pynde | ditto |
| 1414 | Henry Archynton | ditto |
|      |       | (1446–8 Robert Radmyld) |
|      |       | (Lord of Lancing) |
| 1482 | Thomas Hogan | Priory of Mottenden |
| 1482 | Thomas Lyne | ditto |
| 1509 | William Robynson | ditto |
| 1511 | William Scameden | ditto |
| 1515 | James Coks | ditto |
| 1515 | John Roger | ditto |
| 1521 | Simon Dawson | ditto |
| 1521 | Nicholas Thomas | ditto |
| 1530 | Sir Symond Dawson | ditto |
| 1539 | Thomas White | (1539–41 Advowson seized |
|      |       | by Thomas Cromwell) |

*continued—*

*continued —*

| Date | Vicar | Patron |
|------|-------|--------|
| 1548 | Nicholas Thomas | Bishop of Lincoln |
| 1554 | Robert Cargill (or Croshyle?) | ditto |
| 1557 | George Forest | Sir Edward Gage |
| 1560 | John Gibbons | Bishop of Chichester |
| 1571 | Walter Gibbons | Bishop of Lincoln |
| 1623 | Thomas Robynson | ditto |
| 1626 | Thomas Bolney | ditto |
| 1639 | Thomas Langridge | The Crown |
| 1645 | Christopher Grace | Bishop of Lincoln |
| 1649 | Thomas Newman, M.A. | ditto |
| 1660 | Thomas Langridge | ditto |
| 1662 | Vicar of Sompting served as minister | (not known) |
| 1671–86 | Bernard Chatfield | ditto |
| 1686–1706 | (not known) | ditto |
| 1706 | Thomas Williams | The Crown |
| 1743 | Edward Martin | Bishop of Chichester |
| 1766 | William Marchant | Bishop of Lincoln |
| 1802 | Robert Briggs | ditto |
| 1808 | Matthew Feilde | ditto |
| 1823 | Thomas Nash | ditto |
| 1834 | Fisher Watson | Bishop of Lincoln |
| 1860 | Fred. Fisher Watson | Bishop of London |
| 1883 | Edmund Peel | ditto |
| 1920 | Edward Curphey Paton | ditto |
| 1933 | George Wells Foster | ditto |
| 1946 | Everard G. K. Esdaile | ditto |
| 1959 | James Nevil Thompson | ditto |
| 1961 | Kenneth T. Toole-Mackson | ditto |

# APPENDIX III

## A LIST OF MAPS RELATING TO LANCING AND THEIR SOURCES

(1) 'A survey of the Coast of Sussex, made in 1587, with a view to its defence against foreign invasion, and especially against the Spanish Armada' (ed. by M. A. Lower), 1870, 26 pp., maps. From an original survey by Sir Thomas Palmere and Walter Coverte, deputy Lieutenants of Sussex. Part of the map shows the coast of Lancing area. A useful book which can be found in most reference libraries.

(2) A map of the salt marshes of Lancing (mainly the area covered by the present Old and New Salts Farms, New Monks Farm, and the Aerodrome), date and surveyor unknown. Date estimated between 1590 and 1610. Contains some very interesting information about the salt marshes but no information on Lancing village. This map is held at the Marlipins Museum, Shoreham-by-Sea. Permission to view obtained only through the curator.

(3) *Lancing and Shoreham, 1622.*

'A plotte of the Salte mershes lyinge on the West Syde of Shoreham haven from Well Dyke to the Stoane beatche . . . the new Inned mershes from the Damm and Sluce att Lawncinge Shopps to Sea Mill and Worthinge Gate', October 1622, by George Randall (no scale, but about 20in. to 1 mile), 18½in. by 32in., irregular. Reference: Petworth House Archives 3263. Permission to view obtainable from the County Archivist of West Sussex, West Sussex Record Office, Chichester. Similar remarks about the contents of the map apply as (2) above.

(4) *Lancing 1770.*

'A survey of the Manor of North Lancing and Monks, South Lancing and Lyons and Sundry Estates belonging to the Hon. Charles Biddulph Esq.', by Thomas Davis of Godalming, 8in. to 1 mile, 53½in. by 26in. This map contains detailed information of all property owned by the lord of the manor (Charles Biddulph) and covers an area from Applesham parish to the sea and from the Sompting boundary to where the river Adur once emptied into the sea at Aldrington. The copy of this map, in the possession of the author, appears to be the one that was used in evidence in the court case Lloyd *v.* Ingram, 1868.

177

(5) *Lancing 1770*

Description as above, but this copy is only the eastern portion of the above map. Contains only fields relating to New Salts Farm and land to the south of the River Adur as far as Aldrington.

Reference: Arundel Castle MS. PM 152.

Permission to view from County Archivist of West Sussex, West Sussex Record Office, Chichester.

(6) *Lancing 1803*

'Plan of the Parish of Lancing on the Division and Enclosure.' Surveyor not named, but in the Award as George Bassett of London Road, Southwark Co. Surrey. About 11.6in. to 1 mile, 32in. by 23in. Reference: W.S.R.O., Par. 118/20/1. Contains detailed information of Lancing,, including field-names. A great deal of information on field-names, etc., can be gained by studying the Award which is complementary to the map.

Permission to view as (5).

(7) *Lancing 1838* (The Tithe Map)

'The Enclosure Plan corrected and the Residue of the Parish surveyed by Messrs. Bassett and Co., Southampton Office, Fitzroy Square', 26.6in. to 1 mile, 59in. by 95in.

Reference: W.S.R.O. TD/W75.

This map together with the Award contains a vast amount of information relating to field-names, occupiers, owners, and buildings in Lancing.

Permission to view as (5). This is an extremely large map and demands a large amount of space for viewing. When planning to view this map advance warning would no doubt be appreciated by the County Archivist.

(8) *Ordnance Survey Maps*

There are a number of Ordnance Survey maps available on Lancing which are extremely useful and are 6in. or 25in. to the mile. The following dates and scales are those which are easier to obtain.

1869 (6in.); 1899 (6in.); 1912 (6in.); North Lancing 1912 (25in.); South Lancing 1912 (25in.); 1931/2 (6in. or 25in.); 1942 (Revision on 25in); South Lancing and North Lancing separate maps.

Some of the 25in. to 1 mile maps are very difficult to find, and one may have to be satisfied with 6in. to 1 mile.

Some locations are as follows: West Sussex Record Office, Chichester; Worthing Reference Library; British Museum. (Copies of 1869, 1899 and 1931, etc., 6in. to 1 mile are obtainable for a fee. A fairly long delay is often unavoidable.)

There are many other county maps which show Lancing but are often small scale and do not contain much information relating to Lancing itself, although some of them show outlines of fields. However, I feel that those outlined above are the most important.

# REFERENCES

## Abbreviations Used in the References

Cartwright: Edmund Cartwright, M.A., F.A.S., *The Parochial Topography of the Rape of Bramber in the Western Division of the County of Sussex*, 1830

Horsefield: Thomas Walker Horsfield, *The History, Antiquities and Topography of the County of Sussex*, 1835.

*S.A.C.: Sussex Archaeological Collections relating to the History and Antiquities of the County*, published by the Sussex Archaeological Society, Barbican House, Lewes.

S.R.S.: Sussex Record Society.

*S.N.Q.: Sussex Notes and Queries*. A quarterly journal of the Sussex Archaeological Society, Barbican House, Lewes.

S.A.S., Lancing Deeds: Deeds relating to Lancing held by the Sussex Archaeological Society, Barbican House, Lewes.

Handford: B. W. T. Handford, *Lancing: A History of SS. Mary and Nicolas College, Lancing 1848-1930*, 1933

Lloyd *v.* Ingram: Transcript of a court case relating to the dispute of boundaries of land south of the River Adur at Shoreham, between Lloyd (lord of the manor of Lancing) and Ingram (lord of the manor of Shoreham) in 1868. Copy of the transcript, in book form, held in the Marlipins Museum, Shoreham.

W.S.R.O.: West Sussex Record Office, County Hall, Chichester.

*V.C.H.: Victoria County History of Sussex*, 'Rape of Bramber' (unpublished at the time of writing this book).

## Chapter One

1. *S.A.C.*, Vol. 81, pp. 142-143.
2. Horsefield, p. 207.
3. *S.A.C.*, Vol. 81, p. 160.
4. *Ibid.*, pp. 170-172.
5. R. G. Roberts, M.A., *The Place Names of Sussex*, 1914.
6. *Place Names of Sussex*, English Place Name Society, Vol. VI (ed. by Mawer and Stenton), part I, p. 200.

7. Feet of Fines, S.R.S., Vols. 2, 5 and 23.

8. Subsidy Rolls, S.R.S., Vol. 56, p. 78.

9. Domesday Book.

10. Subsidy Lists, S.R.S., Vol. X, p. 61.

11. *Ibid.*, p. 162.

12. *Ibid.*, p. 276.

13. Cartwright.

14. Post mortem Inquisitions, S.R.S., Vol. III, No. 49.

15. S.A.S., Lancing Deeds.

16. Protestation Returns, S.R.S., Vol. V, p. 111.

17. Lloyd *v.* Ingram.

18. Although it was believed that most of the 17th and 18th century records were possibly destroyed in fires in 1739 and 1826 at the lord of the manor's house in Burton Park, the transcript of a court case of 1868 showed that these court rolls were produced as evidence during the proceedings. From that point I have traced them until the early part of this century, when James Martin Carr-Lloyd in 1907 sold land to the Shoreham and Lancing Land Co. At that time he signed a declaration acknowledging his responsibility as lord of the manor for the safe keeping of the manor rolls, but from then on they seem to have been lost.

19. 'A Survey of the Manor of North Lancing and Monks, South Lancing and Lyons and Sundry Estates belonging to the Honourable Charles Biddulph Esq., in the Parish of Lancing in the County of Sussex, 1770'. Surveyed and delineated by Thomas Davis of Godalming in Surrey (in the possession of the author).


**Chapter Two**

1. W. D. Parish, *Domesday Book in relation to the County of Sussex*, published in 1886.

2. *V.C.H.*

3. *V.C.H.* (Westm. Abbey mun., 5469, ff. IV, 27v; *Cur. Reg. R.* IV, 242, 304; v. 27).

4. *V.C.H.* (Westm. Abbey mun. 5469, f.1).

5. Cartwright, p. 40.

6. *S.A.C.*, Vol. 105, p. 81.

7. *S.A.C.*, Vol. 82, p. 26; Cartwright.

8. Chichester Chartulary (S.R.S., Vol. XLVI, p. 376).

9. *V.C.H.* (Westm. Abbey Mun. 5469, ff. IV, 27v).

10. *V.C.H.* (C.P. 40/129, ro. 146; Westm. Abbey mun. 4072, 5469, ff. IV, 27v; *cf. ibid.* f.1).

11. *S.N.Q.*, Vol. IV, p. 236.

12. *V.C.H.* (*Cal. Inq. Misc.*, 1, p. 274; *Plac. de Quo Warr.* [Rec. Com.], 754).

13. Cartwright, p. 41 (from an original communicated by William Bray, Esq.).

14. Cartwright, p. 41 (Ped. fin. 8 Edw. II).

15. *S.A.C.*, Vol. 15, p. 15.

16. *V.C.H.* (*Cal. Inq. p.m.*, XI, p. 143; C 143/338/18); Cartwright (Inq. ad q.d. 35 Edw. III).

17. *V.C .H.*

18. *S.A.C.*, Vol. X, p. 139; *V.C.H.* (C137/163/21; Feud, Aids, VI. 524).

19. *V.C.H.* (e.g. C139).

20. S.R.S., 'Feet of Fines for the County of Sussex', No. 3319, p. 293.

21. William Berry, 'County Genealogies, Pedigrees of the Families in the County of Sussex', 1830, p. 138.

22. *S.N.Q.*, Vol. X, p. 139.

23. S.R.S., Vol. XIX, p. 260.

24. *V.C.H.*

25. S.A.S., Lancing Deeds, Ref. S, Nos. 256 and 259.

26. *S.A.C.*, Vol. XXVIII, p. 167 (British Museum, Burrell MSS.).

27. John Evans, 'A Picture of Worthing', 1805.

28. S.A.S., Lancing Deeds, Ref. S, Nos. 265-268 inc.

29. Lloyd *v.* Ingram.

30. The 'Right of Wrecks' was a term used by the historian Cartwright to define a privilege which was often granted to the lords of the manor by the Crown. (Under Common Law any wrecks, cargo or portions of the cargo from the wrecks which were washed up on land became the property of the Crown—*The Dictionary of English Law* [ed. by Earl Jowitt], 1959).

31. Extracts of Court Rolls taken from Lloyd *v.* Ingram.

32. Cartwright.

33. S.R.S., Vol. 59, p. 100.

34. *S.A.C.*, Vol. XL, p. 113.

35. *V.C.H.* (Sussex Fines, 1509-1833; ii [S.R.S. xix], 148).

36. W.S.R.O., Add. MSS. 19563.

37. S.A.S., Lancing Deeds, Ref. S, No. 229.

38. S.R.S., Vol. XXXIII, No. 215, p. 59.

39. *Ibid.*, No. 247, p. 272.

40. *V.C.H.* (Sussex Fines, 1509-1833; ii [S.R.S. xx], 394; *cf.* W.S.R.O., M.P. 1336, ff. 2-3).

41. *V.C H.* (E.179/258/14, f. 17; *cf. Complete Peerage.* ix 45-7).

42. *V.C.H.* (W.S.R.O., Add MSS. 10381-3).

43. S.A.S., Lancing Deeds, Ref. S, No. 260.

44. *Ibid.*, No. 255.

45. W.S.R.O., Land Tax records relating to Lancing.

46. *V.C.H.* (W.S.R.O., Add. MSS. 3859, 3861).

47. *V.C.H.* (Bk. of Fees, ii. 690).

48. *V.C.H.* (*Chich. Acta.* [Cant. and York Soc.], p. 139).

49. *V.C.H.* (E.326/1681).

50. Cartwright (*Placita de Juratis et Assisis*, 7, Edw. I).

51. Cartwright.

52. *V.C.H.* (Elwes and Robinson, *W. Sussex* 264 n).

53. *V.C.H.* (C54/474, No. 37).

54. S.R.S., Vol. XIV, No. 939.

55. *V.C.H.* (E134/34 and 35 Eliz. Mich. 17, m.4).

56. *V.C.H.* (E 308/4/33, ro. 6).

57. S.A.S., Lancing Deeds, Ref. S, No. 230.

58. *Ibid.*, No. 231.

59. *Ibid.*, No. 233.

60. *Ibid.*, Nos. 236 and 237.

61. *Ibid.*, No. 246.

62. *Ibid.*, Nos. 248 and 249.

63. *Ibid.*, No. 256.

64. *Ibid.*, No. 258.

65. *Ibid.*, No. 262.

66. *Ibid.*, No. 264.

67. *Ibid.*, Nos. 266 and 267.

68. 'Place Names of Sussex', *English Place Name Society* (ed. by Mawer and Stenton), Vol. VI, pt. I, p. 200.

69. B. W. T. Handford, 'Lancing in the time of Elizabeth I', *Lancing College Magazine.*

70. Henry Cheal, 'The Story of Shoreham', 1921.

71. S.R.S., Vol. XXXIII, No. 137.

72. *Ibid.*, No. 181.

73. S.A.S., Lancing Deeds, Ref. S, Nos. 344–361 inc.

74. S.R.S., Vol. X, p. 62.

75. *S.A.C.*, Vol. 98, p. 55.

76. *V.C.H.* (Sussex), Vol. IV, p. 91.

77. Deeds held by Worthing Borough Council, File A42.

78. *S.N.Q.*, Vol. XV, p. 150.

79. *S.N.Q.*, Vol. IV, p. 183.

80. *S.N.Q.*, Vol. X, pp. 162 and 276.

81. *S.N.Q.*, Vol. XXIII, p. 53.

82. *S.N.Q.*, Vol. VI, pp. 203 and 4.

83. *S.N.Q.*, Vol. X, p. 276.

84. *S.A.C.*, Vol. 27, p. 85.

85. 'A plan of the salt marshes' held in the Marlipins Museum, Shoreham.

86. Petworth House Archives, No. 3263, 'A Plotte of the Salt Marshes . . .'.

87. Palmer and Covert's Survey of the Sussex Coast, 1587 (ed. by Mark Antony Lower), 1870.

88. Lloyd *v.* Ingram, 1868.

89. *S.A.C.*, Vol. 90, p. 155.

90. S.A.S., Lancing Deeds, Ref. S., No. 68.

91. *Ibid.*, No. 448.

92. *Ibid.*, Nos. 449 and 450.

93. *Ibid.*, Nos. 453 and 454.

94. Worthing and District *Blue Books and Directory*, 1912–1940; *Kelly's Directory of Worthing*, 1940–1953.

95. W.S.R.O., Land Tax records relating to Lancing, 1780-1832.
96. *S.A.C.*, Vol. 24, p. 245, note.
97. W.S.R.O., Copy of the particulars and conditions of sale.
98. S.R.S., Vol. 56, Lay Subsidy Rolls, 1524-5, p. 78.
99. S.R.S., Vol. 5, West Sussex Protestation Returns, 1641, pp. 111-12.
99a. S.A.S., Lancing Deeds, Ref. S, No. 97.
99b. Ret. Av. Reg. (Rec. Com.) (ii), 271 East. 1200.
100. Cartwright.
101. *S.A.C.*, Vol. XII, p. 41.
102. S.R.S., Vol. XIV, No. 506.
103. *Ibid.*, No. 148.
104. S.A.S., Lancing Deeds, Ref. S., No. 31.
105. *Ibid.*, No. 55.
106. *Ibid.*, No. 75.
107. *Ibid.*, No. 88.
108. *S.A.C.*, Vol. XXV, p. 200; W.S.R.O., Land Tax Records.
109. S.A.S., Lancing Deeds, Ref. S., No. 102.
110. *Ibid.*, No. 43.
111. *Ibid.*, No. 95.
112. *Ibid.*, No. 53.
113. *Ibid.*, No. 62.
114. *Ibid.*, Nos. 70 and 71.
115. W.S.R.O., Par. 118/201.
116. S.A.S., Lancing Deeds, Ref. S., Nos. 92-94.
117. *Ibid.*, No. 40.
118. *Ibid.*, No. 96.
119. *Ibid.*, No. 50.
120. *S.N.Q.*, Vol. IV, p. 235.
121. Cartwright (Inq. ad. q.d. 35 Edw. III).
122. *S.N.Q.*, Vol. IV, p. 235.
123. S.R.S., Vol. XLVI, p. 377.
124. *V.C.H.* (*Cal. Pat.* 1547-8, 154).
125. *V.C.H.* (B.L. Add. MSS. 39461, f. 141).
126. Cartwright and *V.C.H.* (W.S.R.O., Ep. I/22/1 [1662]).
127. *V.C.H.* (B.L. Add. MSS. 39477, f. 68v).
128. Cartwright.

**Chapter Three**

1. *The Dictionary of English Law* (ed. by Earl Jowitt), 1959.
2. S.R.S., Vol. XLIX, p. 93.
3. S.R.S., Vol. V, p. 111.
4. S.A.S., Lancing Deeds, Ref. S., No. 229.
5. *S.A.C.*, Vol. I, p. 59.
6. Used by Mr. B. W. T. Handford for articles on Elizabethan Lancing in the *Lancing College Magazine* during the 1950s.

7. One held at the Marlipins Museum, unsigned and undated, but thought to be *c.* 1590, showing marshland at Lancing. The other map was drawn by George Randall in 1622 (Petworth House Archives, 3263) and shows similar areas.

8. W.S.R.O., Add. MSS. 19,563 and 4.

9. Cartwright.

10. Information from the accounts book of Lady Elizabeth Lloyd (at present temporarily in the possession of the author).

11. W.S.R.O., Add. MSS. 19,569.


## Chapter Four

1. *V.C.H.* (W.S.R.O., MF 48, f. 10v).

2. I am indebted to Miss Wright, great grand-daughter of Robert Wright, for the early information on Lancing Grammar School.

3. Printed particulars of sale of property at South Lancing, etc., S.A.S., Lancing Deeds, No. ND 126.

4. L. W. Cowie, *A Dictionary of British Social History*, 1973.

5. W.S.R.O., E.118 D/6/1.

6. W.S.R.O. Par 118/25/4.

7. *V.C.H.* (Return of Schs. 1893 [*c.* 7529]. p. 602, H.C. [1894], 1xv).

8. *Worthing Herald*, 14 September 1973.

9. In the author's possession.

10. S.A.S., Lancing Deeds, Ref. S., No. 37.

11. Worthing Reference Library, general file on Lancing's history.

12. *Lancing: A History of SS. Mary and Nicolas College, Lancing 1848-1930*, 1933.

13. Much of the information for this article is taken from a small pamphlet entitled *Lancing Works*, published by the Southern Region of British Rail (1962 edition), copies of which were available on open days.


## Chapter Six

1. S.R.S., Vol. X, p. 61.

2. *Ibid.*, p. 162.

3. *Ibid.*, p. 276.

4. S.R.S., Vol. 56, p. 78.

5. S.R.S., Vol. V., pp. 111-12.

6. S.R.S., Vol. XLIII (*Sussex Wills*, Vol. III).

7. *V.C.H.* (E.179/189/42, m. 21).

8. *V.C.H.* (S.P. 12/39, No. 11, f. 29).

9. Cartwright and *V.C.H.* (W.S.R.O., Ep. i/26/3, f. 15).

**Chapter Seven**

1. Extract from the *Sussex Weekly Advertiser*, 1 June 1789.
2. Poster, dated 1797, held in the reference section of Worthing Library.
3. S.A.S., Lancing Deeds, Ref. ND. 128.
4. *Ibid.*, ND 124.
5. Handford, p. 304.
6. Most of the early information on the present Lancing Football Club was obtained from the *Lancing Athletic Football Review* of 1948 by kind permission of the author of the article, Mr. Roy Downing.

# INDEX